From Sources to Citation

A Concise Guide
to the Research Paper

Richard Charnigo

Cuyahoga Community College

HarperCollins*CollegePublishers*

Acquisitions Editor: Patricia Rossi
Project Coordination and Text Design: Ruttle Graphics, Inc.
Cover Design: Kay Petronio
Art Studio: Ruttle Graphics, Inc.
Electronic Production Manager: Angel Gonzalez Jr.
Manufacturing Manager: Willie Lane
Electronic Page Makeup: Ruttle Graphics, Inc.
Printer and Binder: Malloy Lithographing, Inc.
Cover Printer: Malloy Lithographing, Inc.

From Sources to Citation: A Concise Guide to the Research Paper

Library of Congress Cataloging-in-Publication Data

Charnigo, Richard.
    From sources to citation : a concise guide to the research paper /
  Richard Charnigo.
        p.   cm.
    Includes bibliographical references and index.
    ISBN 0-673-99691-3
    1. Report writing.   2. Research.   I. Title.
  LB2369.C474   1996
  808'.02--dc20   95-4156
                                                            CIP

        98 9 8 7 6

Contents

Chapter 6

Chapter 7

Preface

Why This Book?

Have you ever brought home an instruction booklet for a lawn mower, VCR, etc. that was written for models 1000, 1100, and 1200 A & B? And you wished that they had just written each one separately so you didn't have to always remember which one of the three (or was it four?) models you had? Research paper books that try to give you every possible variation in style, method, or approach are like that—300 pages of material when what students really need is a book tailored to their immediate needs, i.e., a first-year college research paper book that concentrates on the research process and not overmuch on the form. Students need enough examples of items that they might really encounter—not the National Union Catalog or the Union List of Serials (sources that they might use in graduate school), but books, newspapers, magazines, journals, pamphlets, data banks, television programs, legal documents, business reports, advertisements, and other materials that they might realistically use now.

The premise of this book is that students need to understand the concept of research before they can write a successful research paper. And the best way to learn research is through a hands-on approach with topics that are doable. Since this book is a first-year college text, it concentrates on those things that a first-year student will need to know, not on those things a third- or fourth-year student will need to know. Doing a research paper is a complicated enough task without adding the obfuscation of unneeded, or very rarely needed, materials. Therefore, students are guided through the research process, and their questions are anticipated and answered as they go through that process. The first part of the text provides familiar examples of what constitutes research, and, as Thomas Henry Huxley did with his explanation of the scientific method, I want to show that people do research all the time informally but do not realize it. I also want to show that with the proper technique, students can do a quality research project.

This text also provides fifty detailed topics that a student can choose from. Each topic consists of a discussion with the student, asking him or her to respond to the questions raised within each topic. Thus the topics become research models, and the student should read and study all the models, not just pick one and forget the rest, because the more reinforcement of the research process, the better it is for the student researcher. The topics cover areas that the student is likely to have some familiarity with (the world of work, entertainment, advertising, consumer goods and services, courses of college study, etc.) or can become expert in in a relatively short time (the stories of Flannery O'Connor, the Toffler trilogy, etc.). This text discourages topics that lessen the opportunity for original research because they require technical expertise of a type that a student might not be able to attain in six to eight weeks or where gaining the necessary familiarity with the materials of the topic would not be possible because of distance or great expense (the nuclear power controversy, construction methods and materials used in building the Alhambra, the apparent mystery of the Bermuda triangle, etc.). To be successful, you have to write about something you know in order to draw inferences and synthesize the information that is discovered.

The best way to become really familiar with the research process is to do original research using primary sources supplemented by secondary sources, rather than the other way around, the latter being the most common procedure but not the most effective because of the inexperience of the researchers and the demands and length of the project. Therefore I suggest a paper of about 1500–1700 words (but not longer than about 2000 words) that will be completed in six to eight weeks. Once the student learns the basic principles, the length then becomes determined by the available time and the magnitude of the project.

This text incorporates changes to the Modern Language Association's style for research papers as specified in the fourth edition (1995) of the *MLA Handbook*. Major changes include emphasis on handling the electronic information sources with which student researchers (and everybody else!) will need to become increasingly familiar.

I would like to acknowledge the support, assistance, and kindnesses of my colleagues in the English Department and library of Cuyahoga Community College, and, likewise, to thank the talented people at HarperCollins and Ruttle Graphics for their help and patience; to my wife, Barbara, thanks, as always, and for everything, and to my son, Rich, who assisted me with a keen eye and a keener insight, I say thanks and thanks again.

Richard Charnigo

Chapter 1

What Is Research?

Sometimes people think that research is simply the gathering of information; it is more than that. Research is discovery, and a research paper is the sharing of that discovery. Think of how much fun it is to discover something: perhaps the answer to a difficult math problem or even a more efficient way to mow the lawn. These are little things, but they still afford us the pleasure of discovery. In a research problem and the paper produced as a result, the rewards are greater. You are like an inventor who comes up with a product that makes people's lives easier and the inventor's life more monetarily interesting! Thus, research implies at least a two-step process: first, you find facts and opinions and then you do something with that information. You analyze it, compare it, classify it, synthesize it, and evaluate it. You simply don't present it (like all the packaged and uncooked ingredients of a stew), but you present it in such a knowing way that you are regarded as an expert on the topic that you are writing about (like a chef who knows how to put all the ingredients together to make a satisfying, substantial, and appealing dish).

What Is Original Research?

First, we should say what *unoriginal* research is. It would be uninspired, would make no discovery, and probably would be a rehash, or what a French chef might call a *réchauffée,* a warmed-over dish. Unoriginal research occurs when the student isn't interested in the topic, doesn't devote enough time to it, and then merely goes over information that was found in three or four sources and presents it uncritically to the reader.

Original research, on the other hand, is unique. Only you have approached the topic this way. It starts from your own natural curiosity because you want an answer to a question that puzzles you. Because you are interested in the topic and the answer, you follow through with your investigation and are eager to present the results to whoever will listen. Eureka!

Thus, original research breaks new ground; it is based upon an idea that the researcher comes up with and pursues in an original way, and the investigation is done primarily by the researcher, not by the authorities consulted. For example, you hear that a new super mall has opened in Minnesota that is the biggest mall in the country, and that gets you thinking: why are shopping malls so popular? And, even more importantly, how have they changed our living habits, to say nothing of our buying habits? Does this growth signal a new type of city, almost totally dependent on the automobile? Is this bigness good? And what of the automobile and its pollution, its contribution to urban gridlock, its expense? You have a lot of questions, and that's good. Now you must see what kind of information you can gather to help you answer the questions you posed. You could find out how many shopping centers there are in the country, how big they are (in area and/or number of stores), and what kinds of stores occupy the malls. You could survey people to find out how often they go to a mall and for what purpose. (You could later compare your findings with regional or national statistics.) You could classify the kinds of stores in the mall—is every kind of business represented or only certain kinds? Can you find out how much it costs to lease space and how long a time commitment you must make to the mall owners? Can you compare several malls to see if they operate similarly? You should also be able to find out comparable information about other malls in the country from your reading of primary and secondary materials.

Having done your preliminary investigation on malls, you might make some hypotheses: that the suburban mall functions as the new suburban downtown, that it has become the new town square, that this sprawl will pose great problems in the beginning of the next century (increasing pollution, foreign energy dependency, alienation, and lack of community, for example) unless we do something about this phenomenon now. You will then have to come up with a thesis statement that encapsulates your hypotheses in a sentence (or two) and that you will demonstrate throughout the paper. Let's collapse what we've said into the following statement:

> The growth of the suburban mall signals an automobile-dependent lifestyle
> that typifies urban alienation and contributes to a lack of community.

Based on what you discovered on your own and what you read in primary and secondary sources, your paper should evolve into an interesting and original assessment of a modern problem from your unique perspective.

Exercise 1.1: Comment on the following examples of research in daily living

1. You are a trusted and experienced employee of a growing insurance firm, and your boss asks you to check out new office space. Should the company buy an existing building, build a new one, lease space in a mini-mall, or stay put for the time being? You have two weeks to come up with some answers and report to your boss. How would you proceed?

2. You see commercials on television encouraging people to lease a new car. You wonder why anybody would lease a car rather than buy a new one and have the equity in it. On what information would you base your answer? Where would you get this information?

3. You want to give a special birthday party for your eight-year-old. How do you go about making this day an extra special fun day that she will remember throughout the year?

Commentary on the Exercise

1. In order to be able to write an intelligent and comprehensive report, you would have to devote sufficient time to the project. You would have to gather data and assimilate it, come to a judgment, and then communicate that judgment to your

boss. Specifically, you might talk to real estate agents about buying or leasing office space, and you might talk to a builder to get some ballpark figures (cost per square foot in your area) on construction costs. You would analyze your company's finances to see what the company could afford to pay for a change in location. You might acquaint yourself with building codes, plat charts, and recent real estate transactions to get a better idea of what you need and what you don't need in the way of facilities and location. You would then compile the data, analyze it, and make your recommendations. You will have written a brief research paper based mainly on primary sources.

2. To determine the feasibility of leasing rather than buying a new car, you would certainly talk to a car salesperson and inquire about the down payment, monthly payment amounts, interest rates, any extra charges, and then do some math on your calculator. You could also check the library for possible articles in newspapers or magazines like *Consumer Reports*. These secondary sources can help you make up your mind as to which is the better deal.

3. You might start by asking your friends and family for ideas about birthday parties. Next, you might check the Yellow Pages to see if anyone specializes in entertaining at children's birthday parties. Then you could check magazine indexes at the local library to see if, perchance, someone has written an article that could give you some ideas. You could also stop in at a fast food restaurant on the way home from the library to see if they provide facilities and services for a birthday celebration.

Types of Sources

As we have seen in the preceding exercises, there are sources that provide the information and opinions which the researcher will use to come to conclusions about a topic. We can characterize these sources on three levels to understand their functions better.

A primary source can refer to a person who provides information as well as to the object—a book or an article—that contains the information. A primary source provides information that has not been evaluated by a second party; it is like gold in ore that needs to be assayed to determine its value. A primary source is a book, article, speech, experiment, song, performance, etc., that is used by a researcher for the original information that it contains. In a sense, the primary source is raw data that has not been evaluated by anyone else. It would be anything that you find out for yourself without the help of a prior researcher/evaluator: for example, information that you locate from government sources, like the *Statistical Abstract of the United States* or the *Occupational Outlook Handbook*; information from legal documents like your state's legal code or the *United States Code Annotated*; the proceedings of the U.S. Congress from the *Congressional Record*; the height of the highest mountain in the U.S. from the *World Almanac*; the date of the first "talking" film from the *Encyclopedia of American Facts and Dates*; quotations from John Steinbeck's *The Grapes of Wrath* and from his *Letters* that explain how he came to write *The Grapes of Wrath*.

A secondary source provides secondhand information (usually someone's opinion on a developed topic); for example, in *The Plug-in Drug*, Marie Winn has written about the negative effects of television on the American family. If you use her ideas, impressions, commentary, statistics, interviews, examples, or conclusions, then you must credit her as the source of the material because, in effect, she handed you the information pre-packaged. As another example, any journal author who analyzes, evaluates, or interprets a short story would be a secondary source (but the short story itself is a primary source) because you are using the subjective response to the story by your interpreter of the source material.

A tertiary source provides information that you receive thirdhand. It is anything that you found out from somebody who found it out from somebody else. As you can see, it's a rather roundabout process. If you were reading an article in *Newsweek*, for example, on American colleges and universities, and the *Newsweek* author quoted a college president on the need for higher academic standards, and you then quoted the college president in your paper, that would be a tertiary source. Obviously, using a great many thirdhand sources doesn't make your paper look original.

But before getting started, you will want to get an idea of what is expected in terms of time commitment, focus of the assignment, and requirements of the course and of the instructor.

"How Much Time Should I Spend on My Research Paper?"

For a paper of about 1500–1700 words and eight cited sources (about 5–6 pages of text), plan on about 40 hours from start to finish (for each additional page or 250 words of text, add about 4 hours).[1] Using a time log can be an effective way to keep track of your project; more importantly, it may actually help you to produce a better paper. Managing one's time effectively is the real key to getting work done; it is admittedly a difficult thing to do, but there are some suggestions that can help. Psychologist Dennis Coon (in the book *Introduction to Psychology: Exploration and Application* 6th ed. St. Paul: West, 1992.), for example, tells us that "the key to any self-management program … [is] accurate record keeping." He points out that the effectiveness of record keeping

> is demonstrated by a study [by Johnson and White (1971)] in which some
> students in an introductory psychology course recorded study time and graphed
> their daily and weekly study behavior. Even though no extra rewards were
> offered, students who were asked to record their study time earned better grades
> than those who were not required to keep records. (210)

---

[1]Over the past several years I have asked students to keep a log of time spent on the research paper—from library work to conducting interviews to writing notes, rough draft, and final product. This research log was totally voluntary: there was no grade for completing or not completing it, since I wanted a realistic assessment of time spent. I told students that their logs would help future students by giving them a ballpark figure to work with—not an artificial time frame. It would show the time that students actually spent on a research paper.

The actual average time spent was 41.4 hours, but some took more time: the highest amounts were 68 and 69 hours—both papers were very detailed projects, and both students had difficulty keyboarding; one student was also an international student whose first language was not English, but by dint of hard work wrote an excellent paper. And some students took less time: there were three whose papers took over twenty but under thirty hours, but this seems like much too little time for a major research project. The real middle range—30–50 hours—accounted for over 81 percent of the students.

Two other factors should be taken into account: keyboarding and organizational skills. If you can use a computer keyboard or type at a rate of 30 words a minute or better, you will save yourself a few hours on the total project. Second, and it almost goes without saying, you can't do a good job if you don't put in enough time, if you procrastinate, or if you work in a harried and fitful fashion. Budgeting your time is a good idea; working a little bit every day is also a good idea since it builds momentum and keeps you sharp. As a matter of fact, once you begin note taking and the rough draft, you should work on your paper at least a little each day because brilliant ideas grow dim without your energizing them by thought and synthesis; it is very easy to forget points that you want to make or connections between materials or authorities after a two-week lapse.

Finally, taking a look at what the whole project entails is a good idea. Read the following checklist (with any modifications your instructor might make) and then keep it handy as you progress throughout the research paper process to see if you are doing what the research assignment calls for.

Checklist for the Research Paper

- Your paper should be analytical or argumentative. It should not be a description (The unique beauty of Monument Valley, Arizona, is a must-see for everyone heading west), a summary (Shakespeare wrote great histories, comedies, and tragedies), a process (With the right kind of equipment, you, too, can detail an old car and make it look new), or a report (Air, water, and ground pollutants: what the government found in Pittsburgh in 1990).

- The final version of your paper should be done on a word processor (or typed) and double-spaced throughout.

- Unless your instructor advises otherwise, your paper should contain about 1500–1700 words of text (this does not include the outline and works-cited page). At any rate, you should not go much over 2,000 words of text. Excessively long papers may be returned ungraded for editing.

- Your outline should be at least one full page (double spaced) and should include a thesis statement at the top of the outline and set apart from it. The thesis should reappear in the text of the paper (perhaps in slightly different form), usually at the end of your introduction.

- Your works-cited page should contain only those references for which you have in-text citations. For an assignment of this length, unless your instructor specifies otherwise, you should have a minimum of eight print sources cited (this does not include interviews or other non-print sources such as television programs, for example).

- Make an effort to use up-to-date sources in your paper since your research should represent the latest word on the topic. Using sources from the current year (or within the last twelve months) demonstrates your awareness that in some fields (like computer science, for example) information that is not recent can be misleading or useless and that the most recent sources (especially from periodicals) can provide essential information not found elsewhere. Likewise, using primary sources shows that you are able to synthesize data and that you are able to think for yourself.

- There should be a balance in your sources (you should not rely on only one or two kinds of sources such as several issues of the same newsmagazine).

- The reader should know where borrowed material begins and ends. Provide a signal (author's name or some accurate and suitable substitute, pronoun reference, beginning of a paragraph, announced example beforehand, etc.) to let the reader know where each borrowed sentence comes from. Remember this rule: *Anything not attributed to someone else is attributed to you*. Will that be clear to the reader?

- It's a good idea to have your rough draft finished a week before your research paper is due so that you can check it over carefully before turning it in.

- Have you kept a log of time spent on your project?

Chapter 2
What Is a Good Topic?

A good topic is one that is interesting in itself because it has wide appeal; is timely; is useful to people; is informative; is new, different, or extraordinary. A pretty good topic may have some or all of these characteristics. By comparison, a weak topic will be lacking most or all of the above traits. If the latter is the case, make your topic interesting! For example, let's say that you want to do a paper on the long-delayed conversion in the United States from the English system of measurement to the metric system. Get a good angle or approach from which to present your ideas. For instance: "Metric Conversion in the U.S.: Let's Convert Yards to Meters in the NFL." Using sports has a built-in appeal to it since so many Americans are familiar with football and follow it with a great deal of passion.

Be Interesting as well as Informative

As a rule of thumb, the more specific and concrete you are, the more interesting your writing will be. As a corollary, the more you localize a topic (from the U.S. to Ohio, Wisconsin, Illinois, to Cleveland, Milwaukee, Chicago, to Parma, Wauwatosa, Mount Prospect, for example, and even to a specific neighborhood within a city), the more opportunity you have for original research and the interest generated by your originality. Let's take another example of how a specific appeal generates interest: since money is so much a part of our lives (I need a raise! Do we have enough money? Can we afford this? Don't be penny-wise and pound foolish!), its incorporation into a topic will increase interest and give you an opportunity for original research.

Another way of creating attention is to give your topic multi-dimensionality. Let's use an environmental topic as an example. With talk of a throw-away society, one wonders where all the disposable items of modern times will go. Will we run out of space to store the garbage? Let's look at some distinct areas we can investigate and then derive some questions from different aspects of the topic:

Topic: Will There Be an Eco-Crisis in the Late Nineties?

Idea #1: What do we call the stuff? Is it garbage, trash, rubbish, or refuse?

Approaches: Are these terms all synonyms or is there a significant denotational difference among them? How do environmentalists, waste management specialists, and city governments define those terms? Is etymological investigation helpful? What kinds of sources–dictionary and otherwise–would clarify these terms?

Idea #2: Since we no longer burn leaves, debris, or garbage at dumps, will we be running out of room to store our refuse? Where will new landfills be located? Will they be welcomed as business opportunities, shunned as eyesores, or protested as pollution spreaders?

Approaches: Where are landfills located and how much does a modern landfill cost? How long will one last? Will leachate contaminate ground water?

Idea #3: Who studies garbage? Is interest in this topic academic, industrial, or environmental? Or is it all three?

Approaches: What data have researchers from the University of Arizona's Garbage Project found about landfills and people's eating and disposal habits? How is this modern archeology similar to or different from classical archeological digs?

Idea #4: Is the public's concern about environmental factors a product of lack of information, misinformation, or "urban folklore"? Is there really a crisis?

Approaches: Are disposable diapers, for example, worse or better for the environment than cloth diapers? Do plastic foam cups, foam "peanuts" used as packing materials, and other modern packaging material pose a disposal problem for landfills?

Idea #5: How does your local community handle garbage? (with gloves, no doubt!)

Approaches: Does your local landfill have a containing mechanism to prevent leachate from infiltrating the ground water? What is the cost to a citizen for a year's worth of garbage disposal?

In the above assortment of ideas, notice how you can expand the topic areas to cover individual aspects that might not seem related but which can have an effect on one another. Notice, also, that topics in argumentative or analytical form create an energy that can be transferred into your paper. As we begin investigating the interrelatedness of the five areas, we will come up with facts, statistics, opinions, predictions, and, when all is said and done, answers to our initial questions. This process is discussed in the following sections.

Start by Asking Questions

The object of research is to make a discovery. In order to discover something, you have to start rooting around, asking questions that you don't fully know the answers to. You may have some ideas, some tentative answers, that you need to examine and test. Remember that all of your ideas will not come together until your research is finished and you have time to add everything up, so to speak, to get the total. But the topic you select and the questions you ask about the topic will get you going in the right direction.

Turn Your Questions into a Working Thesis

Since the thesis, the containing statement for the discovery you will make in your paper, is so central to what you are doing, let's look at the process of generating a thesis. The thesis itself is not a question, but it may be derived from one (Why is the sky blue?—Sir James Jeans; Why does the sky get dark at night?—Bruce Bliven; Why don't people grow to be sixty feet tall?—J.B.S.

Haldane). The thesis should not be too general, too simple, or too obvious. For example, football is an exciting sport; movies are too violent; Americans watch too much TV. Rather, a thesis should be specific, definite, and sufficiently complex. (Though television has been called "chewing gum for the eyes," it succeeds best in the non-entertainment area: news, documentaries, and interview programs.) Sheridan Baker says that a thesis should have an "argumentative edge" to it. (Denim jeans are more than a garment; they are a political, social, and cultural statement firmly rooted in the American tradition.) A thesis should make a claim of some sort. (Since crime and educational attainment are linked to socio-economic status, increasing the size of the middle class is important to a stable America.) And, finally, the thesis is important because everything in the paper issues forth from the thesis, and, like a boomerang, everything in the paper comes back to the thesis statement.

At the beginning of your research and after you've done some investigation, you should be able to come up with a hypothesis, a plausible research stance that requires testing. As your time and study progress, your hypothesis may change because of new information (or you may have to throw it out because it failed the test). With some modification and augmentation, then, the hypothesis will turn into a working thesis and then, later, into your final thesis statement.

Before you select your topic, though, read through the entire fifty topics that follow; that way you'll get a better idea about what questions to ask and what is meant by original research and by primary and secondary sources.

Research Paper Topics

The following list of topics contains opportunities for original research using primary sources and then supplemented with secondary sources; select one of the following topics and then narrow it down and tailor it to your specific needs and interests:

1. The five-day work week became standard for government workers in about 1932 and then for others afterward. The American Federation of Labor (AFL), as a matter of fact, advocated a six-hour day along with a five-day work week in 1933. The forty-hour work week went into effect in 1940. Focusing on your state, do you see any changes in the work day/week as we approach the year 2000 and beyond? In this analytical paper, you will want to list the causes and effects of change on the American workstyle. Do this even before you start investigating because you will want to know what *your* ideas are before you see what other people's ideas are. Give all of this some careful thought. Write your ideas down. Then begin your investigation.

2. How funny is funny? Chart the number of "laugh opportunities" on a comedy program, like *Murphy Brown, Seinfeld,* or *Home Improvement,* and compare the results to comparable programs of a generation or so ago, like the *Mary Tyler Moore Show,* the *Andy Griffith Show,* or *Leave It to Beaver.* (You might note as you watch them that *Murphy Brown* and *Mary Tyler Moore* have many stylistic similarities—this could turn into a paper by itself!) After you do your own research and take notes, observe the basic rule for comparative analysis—the bases, or points, of comparison should be the same for the items being compared—and come to tentative conclusions, and then read some primary sources on the programs (what the actors had to say about the series, how books and philosophers define what "humor" is, etc.). After this, read some secondary sources to see how others view these programs and how

funny they feel them to be and how they would assess their importance in our own popular culture.

3. What jobs are available for people in your area? Search out primary sources like newspaper want ads, job-availability lists from employment bureaus, the *Occupational Outlook Handbook* for job listings on a national level now and in the future. How do local figures compare with national figures? As a way of using a multi-level approach, consider the role and influence of labor unions (what percent of the work force is unionized, for example?) and the shift from blue-collar to white-collar jobs. Can you come up with *your own list* of the top ten jobs for the 21st century?

4. What makes a fad catch on? Indeed, fads have been around for a long time, but increasing technology probably accounts for more in the last fifty years than ever before. Consider the Slinky, Rubik's cube, the Barbie doll, pet rocks, Frisbees, the "I ♥ _____" signs and bumper stickers, Wacky Wallwalkers, PBS's Barney, and many more. What prompts people to go along with a fad? Why do some fads catch on and others become duds? You would probably want to start by cataloging the various fads and seeing what they have in common and what their appeal is to. A multi-level approach would take you into the realm of psychology and group behavior, into the study of signs and symbols (semiotics), as well as into advertising and popular culture.

5. Read children's books and take notes on the types of characters that are portrayed in them, the plots used, and the themes developed. How, for example, are male and female roles portrayed in these books? A sufficient number of books will have to be used—perhaps fifty or more—so that your conclusions have some validity. (Note: many children's books are small with large type!) Since you can't always get a representative sample of books (libraries discard old books, so you may not have a historical perspective in your study), you might want to focus on a certain kind of theme: animals as characters, teaching books, puzzle books, pictorial books, books that advance a social agenda, etc. *See also the next topic.*

6. Read all the books of one author and assess their importance as conveyors of culture, knowledge, and entertainment. You would have to choose an author whose books you could get through in a reasonable amount of time. Dr. Seuss and Beatrix Potter and other children's authors are examples where this would be possible. It is also possible with other authors such as Flannery O'Connor, Ralph Ellison, or Henry David Thoreau, whose output is not as extensive as more prolific writers. Also, authors who have written trilogies can be studied because you can concentrate solely on the works in the trilogy, such as *Future Shock* (1970), *The Third Wave* (1980), and *Powershift* (1990) by Alvin Toffler.

7. Explain the importance of logos or commercial symbols for business and/or fashion. Alison Lurie pointed out that clothing labels were customarily inside, but when modern technology made it possible to produce clothing in great volume and good quality at a moderate price, "labels" were placed on the outside to let people know how expensive an article of clothing was. What do you think of that? Do you think designer clothing is worth more than regular clothing? From an artistic point of view, what makes a good logo or symbol?

8. Do you foresee a lengthening of the school day and/or the school year as a means of addressing educational, social, and economic problems in your local area? Will this be a national trend? Using a multi-level approach, consider what such a plan would do for learning: would learning increase substantially to make the extra time and money worth the

change? What would this plan do for family life: would it provide a better, safer, and cheaper environment for children after school and during the summer than the present system? How would this plan be paid for: would it be cost efficient? For some primary sources, check into a local school system's financial report. You can extrapolate costs from teacher salaries, local utilities costs, etc. There will be many secondary sources, but make your mind up first, *before* you look at them. Then compare what others say with what your feelings are.

9. Read a book that has been around for some time. How has the passage of time affected the book's stature? How important has the book become to our culture? Has it attained "classic" status? Why would you (or would you not) consider it a classic? Do other people consider it a classic? Incorporated into your paper should be a definition of "classic literature." Your own definition is important, of course, but so are others', and you will want to make theirs a part of your investigation. How do the early reviews of the book compare to today's critical estimates of the book? How do you account for any divergence of opinion, if there is?

10. What is your assessment of beverage-container deposit laws? Where does your state stand on this issue? Where do *you* stand on this issue? How many states have deposit laws? Do you know anyone from a state with recycling laws? Although a research paper is not a process paper, you will have to explain how such a deposit process works—its good points and drawbacks—so as to analyze the problem effectively. Also, analyze the arguments for and against. How convincing are they? Ultimately, explain how this is a conservation issue, a business issue, and an employment issue. This multi-level approach will add interest to your paper as well as depth.

11. What is the environmental impact of road salt on the urban infrastructure—specifically the snowbelt states (sometimes unflatteringly called the rust belt)? Where would you find primary sources for such a topic? Are there any salt mines in the area? How much does road salt cost? How does salt melt snow? Are there other ways to make driving safe? For a topic like this, which looks difficult at first, it is a good idea to list as many questions as you can; that will give you some ideas for, or approaches to, writing your paper. Where will you locate secondary sources for this topic?

12. Interest in collectibles has produced a fast-growing industry. How long will this interest continue, and what propels it? Assess a particular collectible area. Primary sources will include price lists, catalogs, and the collectibles themselves. Getting in-depth, secondary sources may be a challenge to the researcher. If this topic is done on only one level—information about collecting certain items—the paper will not be as interesting (or as complete) as if the topic were developed on a multi-level basis. For example: why do people collect things in the first place? Does collecting afford some security to the collector? Compared to gold, securities, and other forms of investment, how do collectibles rate? How big a factor would forgeries be?

13. Is franchising a good idea? Investigate the investment possibilities for a certain type of franchise and study the local area market. You might check the Yellow Pages for a listing of fast-food restaurants, for example. You can also look at other aspects of the restaurant franchise—nutrition, packaging and its effect on the environment, etc.—to see what you can come up with that will be suitable for your study. *Entrepreneur* magazine would be a good source for statistical information (primary) and articles about franchises (secondary).

14. Evaluate your state's lottery. Should the state be involved in gambling? Why does Ohio, for example, put the following message on its tickets: "Compulsive gambling can be treated. If you or someone you know has a gambling problem, call the Gambling Hotline 1-800-589-9966." (The preceding quotation is an example of a primary source.) Compared to other games of chance, is the lottery a "better bet"? Is the lottery a form of taxation? If so, is it progressive or regressive? Don't simply explain *how* the lottery works, but examine all aspects of it and then evaluate it.

15. Is there a local ethnic tradition that has enough unique about it to warrant a research study? Don't simply write about how a holiday dinner is prepared and what it means to you, but really examine the history, customs (and perhaps what contributed to the custom—a plenitude of a certain kind of food, for example), entertainments, songs, rituals, etc. of the group. You might also read sources like Edward T. Hall on proxemics (the study of spatial relationships and their effects on people)and Desmond Morris on territorial behavior to see if certain customs and mannerisms allow you to draw inferences and come to conclusions about your region. Concentrate on answering some probing questions and coming up with an interesting, informative, and pertinent thesis statement.

16. Show how a specific and comparatively non-major invention changed our lives in ways we did not expect or could not foresee. This type of paper would be causal analysis that could easily move into argumentation. For inventions, you could look into the *World Almanac* or other reference books that might have more detailed listings of inventions through the ages. Once you've selected the invention, you will have to determine the effects—intended or not—that that invention brought about. Look at immediate effects, remote (almost hidden from view) effects, and short- and long-term effects. You could follow the invention through the years through primary sources to see if there were any modifications or improvements on the product. Examples that would fit this assignment would be the bicycle, Styrofoam cups and packaging, Post-it notes, etc.

17. How does the medium affect the message? Compare a movie with the play it was based on: *Hamlet* is a good example. Inevitably there will be changes that affect how we understand the meaning of the transmuted work. Other comparisons are possible: a book with a movie (*Shoeless Joe* was made into *Field of Dreams*). Soap operas were originally radio plays that made the transition to television as relatively low-budget dramatic series. This is a speculative paper, and your speculations (based on sound inferences) are what will make your paper interesting. (See also the work of Marshall McLuhan, the author of the famous quotation "the medium is the message," as a secondary source in this area.)

18. Students are often experts in contemporary culture because they participate in its formulation. Writing from the perspective of an ethnomusicologist, classify the music types that are important to today's culture and assess their influence. Does music, indeed, "soothe the savage breast" (Congreve's lines are sometimes misquoted, with music soothing the savage "beast"), or does it corrupt both the culture and the hearing of the audience?

19. Take a relatively popular short story, like D.H. Lawrence's "The Rocking-Horse Winner" (British) or Sherwood Anderson's "I'm a Fool" (American), that is more than forty years old and that deals with money in an important way in the story. Then bring the monetary system up to date; in other words, translate the monetary amounts used in the story into today's dollar equivalents. How would you do this? How would your findings help the modern reader to understand and enjoy the story more?

20. Why have westerns declined in popularity? Check the television listings from the 1950s and you will find an abundance of westerns on TV. Check the movie listings from the 1920s through the 1960s and you will see that the western is one of the staples of American movie entertainment. Nowadays, except for reruns and an occasional movie, the western is virtually absent. Why? Are there causative societal factors that can explain this phenomenon? Will the western make a comeback? What will make this paper effective and interesting is a thoughtful, speculative approach that is the result of a carefully sculpted thesis statement.

21. Evaluate the concept of coincidence in fiction and in mathematics. First, you will need a good definition of the term. Check a few dictionaries and see how their definitions compare. Then you can consult a short story text, like Laurence Perrine's *Story and Structure,* to see how the author defines the term as it applies to literature. How much, if any, coincidence is acceptable in a short story? Then consult a mathematical work, like John Allen Paulos's *Innumeracy.* How frequently does coincidence occur: for example, two people having the same birth date? Then synthesize your findings after consulting a sufficient number of primary and secondary sources.

22. Take an event that happened 20–50 years ago, read the original accounts (primary sources) in newspapers and magazines (on microfilm), and compare those accounts with what is written about it in retrospect today. How has time affected our perceptions? Have interpretations changed over the years? (If you don't already, you will have to know how to use the microfilm readers in the library; some machines will even print out a page for a small fee.) An example of a few topics that would fit this assignment would be the introduction of the ENIAC computer, the Marshall Plan, the *Brown v. Board of Education* decision, the launching of Sputnik, and the Cuban missile crisis.

23. Analyze the research position or positions of a person over a number of years on a given topic. For example, if you've had some course work in psychology, you may wish to analyze the work of Jay Belsky on day care to see how and why his ideas have changed over time in this area. Or you may wish to analyze the work of J.S. Wallenstein as to how and why her ideas on the effects of divorce upon children have changed in the last decade. Another possible topic would be to analyze the changes in the moral development theory of Lawrence Kohlberg.

24. Take a type of literature (science fiction, detective stories, westerns, sports stories, etc.) and explore how the genre developed, what attracts people to it, and what it says to and about its readers. Let's use detective fiction as an example. Edgar Allan Poe is regarded as the father of the modern detective story (check out M. Dupin of "The Purloined Letter" as the intellectual detective par excellence). Wilkie Collins, a contemporary of Charles Dickens, is credited with writing the first detective novel, *The Moonstone,* a reading of which repays its leisurely Victorian prose style. And, of course, Arthur Conan Doyle's Mr. Sherlock Holmes, the world's foremost consulting detective, is the exemplar of the classic sleuth. If you are familiar enough with the genre to begin with, read some more, make some hypotheses, read what other observers have to say, and then formulate a thesis statement that answers some of the puzzling questions you started out with.

25. Assess the strength of a local business or industry (what's the difference between a business and an industry, anyway?) like Murphy's Oil Soap, American Greetings, Sherwin-Williams,

Smucker, TRW, etc. Take a look at year-end reports and other primary materials. How does the business/industry fare when it is compared to national or international companies of the same type? *Fortune* and other national magazines would be good secondary sources to use as well as regional and local publications.

26. Could it happen again? On October 30, 1938, Orson Welles's Mercury Theater broadcast an updated version of H.G. Wells's *The War of the Worlds* on the radio that scared the daylights out of people who thought Martians were invading New Jersey. Listen to a tape of the radio play (primary source), read accounts in the New York newspapers of the next day, Halloween (a primary source on microfilm), and read retrospective comments by John Houseman, a radio actor in the play (another primary source). What caused all this to happen? Could anything like this happen today? How? What do you think caused this phenomenon?

27. Check advertising in magazines, newspapers, on television, or radio to see what conclusions you can come to about specific aspects of it. For example, how are men, women, boys, or girls portrayed in advertisements? What devices, like color, sound, graphics, personalities, etc., are used by advertisers to compel people to watch commercials or read ads? Are there any differences in commercials that are 15, 30, or 60 seconds long? Do you think half-hour "infomercials" are effective? In the past twenty years or so, the actual non-commercial time (i.e., actual program time) of a half-hour program has gone down to just over twenty minutes. Does this make you wonder what the purpose of television is?

28. Do a population study of your city and determine the effects of population change on education, real estate, business, city services, political representation, etc. You will want to use the latest figures and compare them to census figures available from decades past. Remember that 1990 was a census year and that there should be considerable information available about how this national census is affecting various states and congressional redistricting within states.

29. Do a study of the popularity of names. Lists of the most popular male and female first names throughout the decades are available from a number of sources. There are also books and journals devoted to the study of names. (*Onomastics* is the word that is used to describe the study of names.) You can, for example, consult lists of first names from yearbooks or other sources where you know that the people are all the same age in a certain category and then tabulate your own popularity list. You can see if your list matches the national listings. You can also examine the controversy over team names and their appropriateness, the reactions of people depicted by the names, and the changes in the culture that gave rise to such objections. But remember that you want to make a discovery, not simply pass on information that you found in secondary sources. In other words, your study develops from a good thesis statement.

30. On May 9, 1961, Newton Minow, chairman of the Federal Communications Commission (FCC), called television a "vast wasteland." He said, "It is not enough to cater to the nation's whims—you must also serve the nation's needs" (qtd. in Carruth 626). Has television improved since Minow's criticism? Check as many primary sources as you can (FCC regulations, National Association of Broadcasters (NAB), television listings of programs, etc.). Then consult secondary sources as you proceed in your assessment of the direction in which television is going.

31. "Everybody wantsta get into de act!"—Jimmy Durante. And everybody wants to be middle class. But what is middle class and why does everyone (even rich people, it seems) want to be in the middle class? What is the political, economic, and social significance of a middle class in a society, and, specifically, ours? Is there an official U.S. Government definition of "middle class" based on household income? See how many different definitions you can come up with; then compare the definitions. How much agreement is there? Keep in mind that if dollar values are given, they will have to be adjusted for inflation. Caution: don't be controlled by secondary sources; remember: this is your study based on evidence that you have collected and synthesized.

32. Can Gustav Freytag's Pyramid, formulated to show the progression and division of dramatic action in a play, be applied effectively to a short story? Is it useful to analyze the structure of a short story? Does the structure contribute to the meaning of a story? Can you demonstrate this by analyzing a short story from a textbook like Perrine and Arp's or X.J. Kennedy's, for example? In your approach to this topic, look up information about Freytag's ideas first, take notes, and then examine your selected story in light of what Freytag says. Then, after you've formulated the substance of your analysis/argument, see what other critics (secondary sources) have to say about your story. Finally, incorporate what they have to say—do you still hold your views, or have they been modified in light of new evidence or opinions?

33. Thomas More coined the term "utopia" when he wrote his novel about an ideal place and used a Greek word (though his book was written in Latin) meaning "no place," indicating, perhaps, the impossibility of perfection on earth. Select a novel from the utopian genre and speculate as to why writers write them, what purpose they serve, and whether you agree with the authors' conclusions. In addition to More's *Utopia,* other examples, but by no means all, of this genre are Edward Bellamy's *Looking Backward,* one of the best-selling books of all time, and William Morris's *The Dream of John Ball.* Some examples of anti-utopias (sometimes called dystopias or negative utopias) are George Orwell's *Animal Farm* and *1984,* Aldous Huxley's *Brave New World,* and William Golding's *The Lord of the Flies.* The object of a paper like this would be literary and critical analysis, an assessment of critics' responses to the work, and your estimate of the artistic achievement of the book. Remember to read primary materials first so you are not swayed by secondary source opinions. Get your ideas down first, and then see what others have to say.

34. Examine the setting of a novel or novella (the setting is the location: jungle, desert, big city, small town, inside the earth, outer space, etc.). Does the setting seem accurately drawn? What part (or role) does the setting play in the story? In some novels, the setting is obviously very important: Steinbeck's *The Grapes of Wrath* (the Oklahoma dust bowl and the trek to California) or Conrad's *Heart of Darkness* (the landscape seems almost impenetrable, and very powerful). In other stories, it is only a backdrop for the interplay of plot and character. You will have to come to at least a tentative conclusion about the significance of the setting (that is, you'll need a tentative thesis statement) before you get too far into producing the paper. Since the thesis controls the direction of the paper, you need this guidance as you collect information and gather others' opinions to stay on track.

35. The present movie rating system—G, PG, PG-13, R, NC-17—has been in effect (with some modifications) since 1968. How well is it working? Would you advocate further modification of the rating system or would you change it entirely? You can survey the movie listings in

the newspaper to see what percentages of variously rated films are playing in the theaters in your area. You might also want to consult Michael Medved's book *Hollywood vs. America* to see what the PBS movie critic has to say about today's films.

36. Use your state's legal code and investigate a law. Is the law "more honor'd in the breach than the observance" (*Hamlet* 1.4.16)? Provide some background and then analyze the situation. For example, you might consider things like helmet laws, safety belt laws, jaywalking laws, etc. You might start with a question like: Is it legal to jog in the street? and then locate the answer in the code. In addition to your state code, other primary sources would include interviews with law enforcement officials, other legal documents like city ordinances, and statistical information. Also, what happens when a law is not enforced? Does it cease to be a law?

37. Watch a sufficient number of cartoons (or other type of television programming) to determine the frequency, duration, and intensity of aggression, sex-role development, stereotypes, etc. Are there any patterns that are evident from your study? What conclusions can you draw from your observations? Compare new cartoons with old cartoons to see if there are any changes evident from past to present. In order to do this assignment, you will need to develop an instrument to mark down observed behaviors and then compile your evidence in a form that can be used to generate conclusions. A sufficient number of cartoons (or other programming) must be watched for you to be able to make valid conclusions.

38. Will we be driving cars in about 30 years? Or will we be riding on monorails, pedaling bicycles, or walking? In other words, what will transportation be like in 2026? Since this is a predictive essay, you will want to support your opinions with facts, statistics, and solid inferential reasoning. You will want to know how many cars are on the road, what fuels will be available, the cost of highway construction and maintenance, what the environmental concerns will be, the role of the automobile in our popular culture, etc. (You might want to read about the Delphi study done by the University of Michigan's Office for the Study of Automotive Transportation.) In order to be successful with this kind of assignment, you will want to know something about the past (the past is prologue) and to be able to project the future.

39. Does television, in general, promote prosocial or antisocial behavior? Examine a certain type of television show (soap opera, situation comedy, police show, etc.) to determine the accurate portrayal of men, women, minorities, nationality groups, family life, occupations, interpersonal relationships, etc. For this type of paper, you will have to spend enough time watching television and taking notes, but before you do this you will have to determine some of the things you will be looking for so that you will know how many and what kind of notes to take. Do a trial run for a couple of days to see what is important enough to talk about.

40. Are local communities protecting the environment sufficiently? Do environmental concerns rest with the federal government alone (through the Environmental Protection Agency) or do local towns and cities have an obligation to enact protective measures for the air and ground and water? To what extent is this being done in your community? How would you locate primary information on this topic? What are the costs for environmental protection? Where is the money coming from? Compare what is being done today with what was done 25 or 50 years ago. This is the kind of topic that requires a lot of research, but the good news is that it is research directed in one area rather than diffused in many directions. This topic may also lend itself to the use of tables. See page 73 for directions about how to compile your data and present it in an attractive and readable format.

41. Are organizations like the Boy Scouts, Girl Scouts, Cub Scouts, and Brownies thriving or declining locally and nationally? For ease in developing your topic, you might want to concentrate on only one group or two groups (Boy Scouts and Girl Scouts, Boy Scouts and Cub Scouts, Girl Scouts and Brownies, Cub Scouts and Brownies), rather than on all four. Have cultural changes had much of an impact on the scouting movement? Look at some old scouting handbooks (primary sources) and old scouting magazines (primary or secondary depending on their use by you): is there much difference between activities of yesteryear and those of today? If you have to write to the organization's headquarters for information or statistics, look in your grammar handbook for information on writing a letter of inquiry and then send your letter off early so that you are not waiting for crucial information that is holding up the progress of your paper.

42. Are "little theaters," or community theaters, getting stronger or weaker? For this assignment, become familiar with a local community theater. From its literature (programs, brochures, etc.), see what kinds of plays are produced. Also, investigate the economic aspects of local theater. Where does the funding come from: local, state, or federal government; private organizations, foundations, businesses; or is the theater self-sustaining? Are the actors paid? How much does a production cost? What sort of revenue is produced in a season? Is the theater run by the city or is it independent? Finally, assess the cultural importance of community theaters to the communities they serve and to the society at large.

43. Examine the effects of technology on society. Some would say that technological advances tend to increase human isolation because we depend less on people and more on things (Daniel Boorstin) and that our pursuit of efficiency frequently has negative human consequences (Jeremy Rifkin); on the other hand, others talk about the liberating effect of technology and one's ability to work out of one's home because of the increasing availability of high-tech communications (Alvin Toffler) and about modern society bringing people together into a "global village" (Marshall McLuhan). How do we sort out all these apparently conflicting consequences of our society's forward progress? Will we be penalized for stepping out of bounds? Or will we achieve our goal of a prosperous future?

44. Do sports build character? Does participation in sports reduce antisocial behavior? Do sports enhance the life of the community? Focus on high school sports or college sports. What role do sports play in education? Take up the question of parity and Title IX. How has the participation of girls and women affected sports and education programs? There is a great body of research that has been done on sports topics. You might consult, for example, the *Education Index,* periodicals such as *Sociology of Sports Journal; International Review of Sport Sociology; Journal of Physical Education, Recreation, and Dance; Journal of Teaching in Physical Education; Sports Illustrated;* and books by H.G. Bissinger and by Andrew W. Miracle, Jr., and C. Roger Rees.

45. Investigate Total Quality Management (TQM) and show how it is being implemented locally. Is this a new way of doing business or has it been in existence for a long time? What role, if any, does W. Edwards Deming play in TQM? Does TQM go by any other names? What is the philosophy of TQM? Will it work for both small and large organizations? Is it a management style that is applicable to business only, or is it being used for other organizations too? Are there any books devoted to this approach to management?

46. Assess the ecumenical movement. Is it making progress locally, nationally, or internationally? Or, in an expanded sense, explore how we are getting along with other world religions.

Is there a movement toward mutual understanding and cooperation among Jews, Christians, Muslims, Hindus, and others? What form does it take? Why does there seem to be so little coverage of religious ideas and events and discussions in the newspaper or in the media in general? Explore what the idea of "separation of church and state" means. Does it mean that the secular media should not discuss religious matters? Michael Medved says that despite the fact that many Americans regularly attend church and synagogue, there is very little evidence of normal religious activity in motion pictures or television. Why?

47. How dependent are we on fast food? For this topic, you might want to gather your own statistics via surveys and interviews. Compare your figures with national figures for things like how often people eat out (or take food out) per week. What are proximate (obvious) and remote (not obvious but important) causes for the continuing popularity of fast food? Try to avoid the obvious or, if you must, deal with obvious reasons in summary fashion; after all, if the reasons are so obvious, then your reader already knows them! Are we adapting to the fast-food industry, or are they adapting to our modern lifestyles?

48. Examine the changes in terminology (melting pot, mosaic, salad bowl, multiculturalism, diversity, etc.) used to express cultural relationships in a pluralistic society. You might, for example, review primary sources by Booker T. Washington and W.E.B. Du Bois, events like the Atlanta Compromise of 1895, the Niagara Movement of 1905, and the formulation of the NAACP to see how the historical framework sheds light on current America.

49. Examine the concept of holidays, vacation days, and/or family-leave days. Explore different cultures as well as our own. Take a look at a calendar and note how many different holidays there are (federal, regional, state, religious, patriotic, etc.). How have the passage of time, the changes in culture, and the force of economics affected their observance? Why are some holidays more popular than others? (Columbus Day is celebrated as Indigenous Peoples' Day in some places, and it has also been known as Discovery Day for many years.) Also, how does the U.S. compare with other countries regarding time off from work (vacation days, family leave, etc.)?

50. Use Aristotle's *Poetics* as a base; then examine either a television program (situation comedy, hour-long adventure show, soap opera, made-for-TV movie, etc.) or a stage play in light of what Aristotle says about drama. Since Aristotle was writing about plays that he saw, what do you think he would say about modern drama, whether on the stage or on television? Is drama universal? Is it the same in each era but differing in minor details that reflect the popular culture of the times? Try to come up with a good angle (thesis) for this topic. The quality of your ideas and their presentation to the reader will make this an engaging paper.

Exercise 2.1: Select two of the 50 topics listed above and, for each, write 100–150 words of discussion, development, and evaluation. Ask questions, speculate on the answers, and try to resolve difficulties. Although it is too early to know exactly what you will do with a topic, some initial brainstorming and idea generation can get you moving in the right direction.

Chapter 3

What the Library Has to Offer

Know Your Library

The library is so important to research that a "research paper" is sometimes called a "library paper." Unless you have a mammoth selection of books, magazines, journals, and newspapers at home and will do field work using a plenitude of primary sources, you will be a frequent visitor to the library.

In the following section is a schematic drawing of a library and its essential features:

The Circulation Desk: Here you check out books and periodicals (and, in some libraries, audio- and videotapes), request books that have been put on reserve by an instructor, and obtain general information about library services.

The Reference Area: In this section of the library, you can find important research tools: the many different kinds of encyclopedias, atlases, music and literary dictionaries, biographies, collections of factual materials, and other useful information. Because of their expense and frequency of use, these books cannot be checked out, but you can photocopy pages that are needed for your study.

Book Catalogs: Whether the library has its books catalogued on index cards, computer-printout books, microfiche, or on computer terminals, the information will be the same. Each type of catalog will list authors, titles of books, and subject areas for each book in the library's collection. The two principal classification systems in use in the United States are the Dewey decimal system and the Library of Congress classification system.

Stacks: These are the stacks of shelved books arranged in groups according to a classification system. For example, the 800s in the Dewey system house all the books on literature.

Periodical Indexes: Because of the rapid advance of technology, there are two kinds of periodical indexes now: those in traditional paper form and those on a database. They function similarly, but the computerized indexes let you work faster and provide much more information. The only drawback to the databases is that they only go back five or ten years, whereas the paper indexes go back fifty to a hundred years.

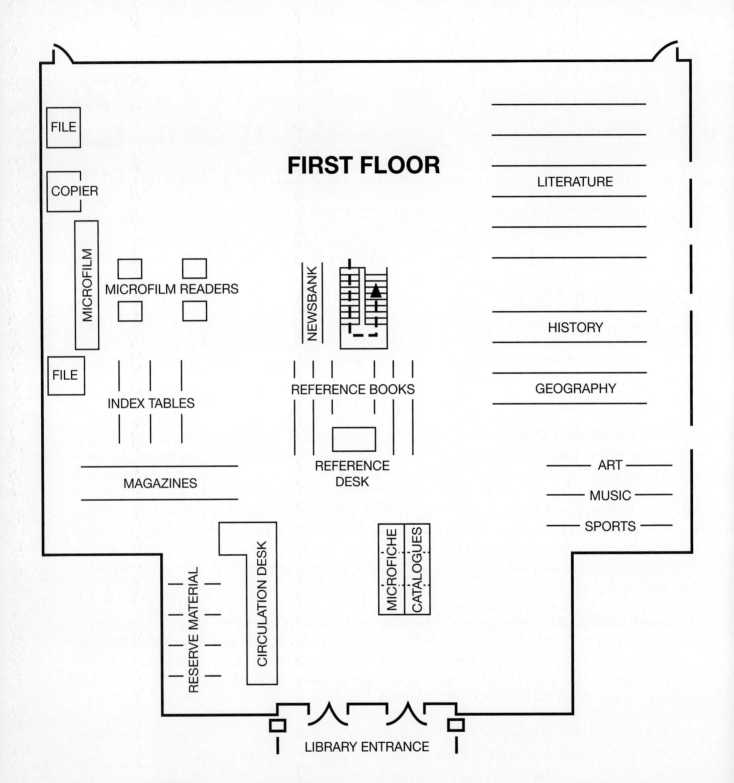

Figure 3.1   Library Configuration

Although libraries will differ in floor plans, they will have these essential elements: a circulation desk, a reference area, periodical collections, shelving stacks containing bound volumes, and the machinery of a modern library: microforms, photocopiers, tape players, and computers that serve a variety of purposes from locating a book to composing a research paper.

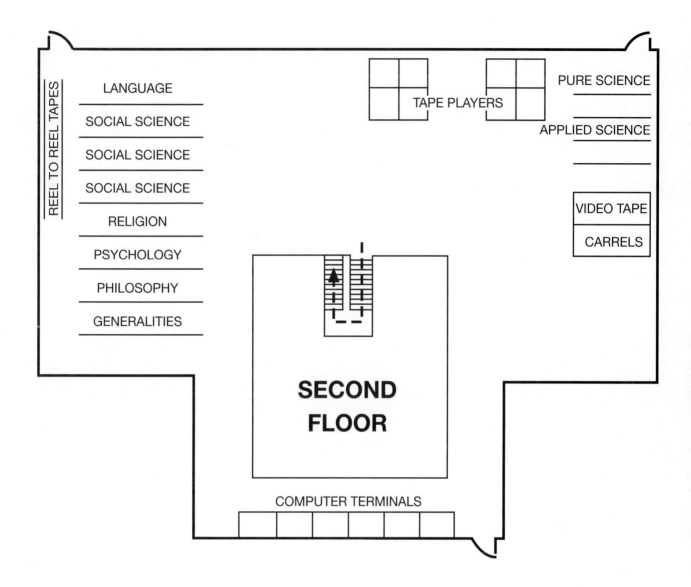

Figure 3.2 Library Configuration (Systematic Arrangement of Books)

The Dewey decimal classification system was invented in 1876 by Melvil Dewey (1851–1931), a librarian at Columbia University and a founder of the American Library Association. The Dewey decimal system classifies books into ten categories that remain the same but that can be expanded linearly. For example, 000–099 is for general works; 100–199 for philosophy and psychology; 200–299 for religion; 300–399 for social sciences; 400–499 for language; 500–599 for natural sciences and mathematics; 600–699 for technology; 700–799 for the arts; 800–899 for literature; and 900–999 for geography and history. Additional numbers and letters after the decimal point further refine the classification by coding the author's last name and distinguishing among other works by the same author.

The Library of Congress classification system uses the letters of the alphabet (omitting I, O, W, X, and Y) for categories ranging from general works (A) to bibliography and library science (Z). As in the Dewey system, additional numbers and letters further refine the system.

Magazine and Journal Racks: These storage shelves house the hard copies of magazines and journals subscribed to by the library. Many libraries only hold recent print copies of periodicals; older copies are contained on microfilm.

Microforms: This is a generic term for any object reduced in size and preserved in a different form and accessed by means of a mechanical device. Microfilm refers to printed pages reduced and placed on spools of film and then read by means of a microfilm reader. A microfiche is essentially the same thing as microfilm, but the reduced pages are contained on a sheet about the size of an index card rather than being on a spool. A microfiche reader is constructed somewhat differently from a microfilm reader, but they both function essentially the same way. Photocopies can usually be made from either device for a small fee per page.

Equipment Available for Student Use: Libraries sometimes provide equipment such as computers and printers, audiotape and videotape machines, photocopy machines, and microform devices.

Reference Books

In the reference area of the library you will find collections of books and individual volumes that can be useful for background information (encyclopedias, almanacs, dictionaries, surveys, etc.) and other works both singly and in collections that can serve as primary sources (state legal codes or the United States Code, for example). Here is a sample of just some of the hundreds of reference books available that you might find in your college or neighborhood library:

New Encyclopaedia Brittanica, 1992 ed., 32 vols.
McGraw-Hill Encyclopedia of Science and Technology, 6th ed., 1987, 20 vols.
Encyclopedia of American Facts and Dates, 8th ed., 1987.
Famous First Facts, 4th ed., 1981.
Facts on File, weekly, 1941–
Encyclopedia of the American Constitution, 1986; 4 vols., 1992, Supp. 1.
Encyclopedia of World Art, 17 vols.
World Encyclopedia of Cartoons, 1983, 6 vols.
New Grove Dictionary of Music and Musicians, 1980, 20 vols.
Oxford English Dictionary, 2nd ed., 1989, 20 vols.
Webster's Third New International Dictionary, 1966 ed.
Dictionary of American Biography, 1990, 10 double vols., 8 supp.
Black's Law Dictionary, 6th ed., 1990.
Black's Medical Dictionary, 36th ed.
Statistical Abstract of the United States, 112th ed., 1992.
Congressional Quarterly Almanac, annually, 1948–
World Almanac and Book of Facts, annually in November
Code of Federal Regulations, 1993, 50 vols.
United States Code Annotated, multi-volume, 1927–
Baldwin's Ohio Revised Code Annotated, 1993, 31 vols.
International Directory of Company Histories, 1991, 5 vols.
Who's Who in America, 47th ed., 1992–93.

The Ninth Mental Measurements Yearbook, 1985 ed., 2 vols.
Magill's Cinema Annual, 1992, 11 vols.
Contemporary Authors, 1993, 138 vols.
Twentieth Century Literary Criticism, 1993, 47 vols.
Critical Survey of Short Fiction, 1981, 7 vols.; 1987 supp.
Short Story Criticism, annually, 10 vols.
Critical Survey of Poetry, rev ed., 1992, 8 vols.
Critical Survey of Drama: English Language Series, 1985, 6 vols.
Contemporary Literary Criticism, annually, 76 vols.
Scholarships, Fellowships, and Loans, 9th ed., 1992–93.

Book Catalogs

When you go into a library and want to find a book (other than a reference book), you head to the card catalog. You may go to large cabinets labeled "Author," "Title," or "Subject," or, increasingly, you may head toward the computer terminal and press F1 for "Author," F2 for "Title," or F3 for "Subject." Either way, the same thing is accomplished, but with computers it will be a lot faster.

Here is information that you might find on an author card or computer printout:

Call number	659.143 B181h
Author	Baldwin, Huntley
Title	How to create effective TV commercials
Edition	2nd ed.
Place, Publisher, Date	Lincolnwood, Ill.: NTC Business Books, 1989
Front matter, text, illustrations, height of book	xii, 286 p. : ill; 26 cm
Notes about book	Rev. ed. of Creating effective TV commercials, 1982
	Includes bibliographical references and index
Subject heading	Television advertising

Figure 3.3   Author Card (Computer Printout)

If you pressed F2 and typed in the title (or something close to it), you would also get the information shown in Figure 3.3. Likewise, if you pressed F3 and typed in the subject word "television," you would get a large list of titles, but narrow the subject to "television advertising," and you would get, perhaps, a dozen titles, one of which would be *How to Create Effective Television Commercials.* Select this title, and once again you would get the information shown in Figure 3.3.

With an on-line computer catalog, you can also call up information as to whether the book has been checked out of the library or if it is still available. You can even place a "hold" on the book by typing in your library card number on the screen. The library's on-line system is a lot like a supermarket's: books are scanned by laser at the circulation desk, that information is fed into the computer, and a "not available" or "available" notation will appear on the screen when the book is called up by the next patron. However, this "hold" feature is not possible on a CD-ROM catalog since information on the disk is "read only," and inventory control, as at a supermarket, is not possible.

Indexes to Periodicals

A periodical is a publication that comes out daily, weekly, monthly, or every few months; in other words, it comes out "periodically"—hence the generic name for newspapers, magazines, and journals.

A periodical index is a listing by subject and by year of articles in newspapers, magazines, or journals. Nowadays, there are two kinds of indexes: those printed on paper and bound in volumes and those "printed" on computer screens and contained in databases. What follows is a list of print indexes that you might find in your library:

Biography Index, 1946–
The H.W. Wilson Company of New York publishes this and many other periodical indexes. This index focuses on biographical information (primarily of Americans) contained in periodicals and books.

Books in Print
The R.R. Bowker Company of New Providence, NJ, publishes this index of books currently in print with listings by author, title, and subject; it also lists publishers as well as books out of print and books out of stock indefinitely.

Book Review Digest, 1905–
This Wilson index lists excerpts of reviews of juvenile and adult literature, both fiction and nonfiction. Excluded from the listing are government publications, textbooks, and technical works.

Book Review Index, 1965–
Gale Research Company of Detroit publishes this index of book review citations (in 1965, for example, there were 116,000 citations of 62,000 books). Some citations also are coded by letters: "r" for a reference work, "p" for periodicals, "c" for children, and "y" for young adults.

Business Periodicals Index, 1958–
This Wilson index covers periodicals that deal with advertising, utilities, and transportation, to name but a few subjects. This work also indexes business-oriented book reviews.

Business NewsBank Annual Index, 1985–
Published by NewsBank of New Canaan, CT, *Business NewsBank* indexes full-text articles of a business nature which have been collected on microfiche.

Cumulative Index to Nursing and Allied Health Literature, 1961–
Published by CINAHL of Glendale, CA, this work indexes about 300 journals and "hundreds" of books from health-field publishers. CINAHL is also available via BRS, DIALOG, and Data-Star as well as CD-ROM.

Education Index, 1929–
This Wilson work indexes articles by author and subject in periodicals that deal with all facets of education. It also contains citations to reviews following the periodical index.

Essay and General Literature Index, 1900–
This Wilson index concentrates on essays *in books* on the humanities and social sciences. According to their prefatory note, this is "an index to 3,785 essays and articles in 324 volumes of collections of essays and miscellaneous works."

General Science Index, 1978–
This fairly recent Wilson index focuses on sciences ranging from astronomy to mathematics to zoology.

International Index, 1907–65
This is the Wilson index that became the *Social Sciences and Humanities Index.* (See the following three entries.)

Social Sciences and Humanities Index, 1965–74
This Wilson periodical index was split into the *Humanities Index* and the *Social Sciences Index* in 1974.

Humanities Index, 1974–
This Wilson index focuses on periodical articles in areas such as the classics, history, literature, and other traditional humanities areas.

Social Sciences Index, 1974–
This Wilson index concentrates on periodical articles in the soft sciences such as anthropology, health fields, law enforcement, psychology, and other related areas.

Reader's Guide to Periodical Literature, 1900–
This Wilson index is probably the most referred to general index. It indexes about 200 periodicals (the volume published in 1990 lists 194, to be exact) of general interest, like *The American Scholar, Atlantic, Better Homes and Gardens, Commonweal, Ebony, National Geographic, Psychology Today, Vital Speeches of the Day,* etc.

MLA Bibliography
This publication of the Modern Language Association of America indexes articles on such major areas as literature, languages, and folklore. This is a valuable index for literary topics.

New York Times Index, 1851–1912 (prior series); 1912– (current series)
This work not only indexes newspaper articles but also gives brief synopses of the articles.

Wall Street Journal Index
This is a Dow Jones publication available from University Microfilms of Ann Arbor, MI, and provides, according to the User's Guide, "abstracts and comprehensive indexing of all articles in the 3-Star Eastern Edition of *The Wall Street Journal.*" This is an excellent source for articles dealing with corporate America as well as for general news.

National Geographic Index, 1888–1988
Published in 1989 by the National Geographic Society of Washington, DC, on the occasion of its centennial, this index lists all articles in the magazine in one volume.

Electronic Indexes

NewsBank Index, 1981–
This index is produced by NewsBank of New Canaan, CT, and covers newspapers from over 450 American cities. This is a microform index updated each month; new articles then appear on microfiche. NewsBank provides the full text of an article, not just the bibliographic details, and covers a wide subject field ranging from art to education to health to science and technology, to name just a few. Because NewsBank reformats the information in the articles, a special works-cited form is needed. (See page 64 for an example and discussion.)

InfoTrac, 1986–
This CD-ROM data base by the Information Access Company provides several groupings of subject matter: a general periodicals index, a business topics index, and a health topics index. This operator-friendly system uses about a dozen keys on the computer keyboard: Function keys (F1–F6) start the database search, provide information about the system, print the data appearing on the screen, get a list of subjects, and go back to previous subjects. The enter key is used to search for other citations, home and end keys move you to the first or last citation, arrow keys move you up or down, etc.

Here are two examples of the type of information you might find using *InfoTrac:*

From the "Health Reference Center–Apr '90–Apr '93" under the subject "Medical colleges" is found this entry:

> The less traveled road to medical school, (nontraditional students apply for
> medical school) by Lisa Belkin il 39 col. in. v141 The New York Times
> June 17 '92 pA1 (N) pA1(L) col 2.

The preceding citations tell us the title, topic, author, size of the article in a newspaper (39 column inches), publication information, page numbers, edition, and location of the article.

From the General Periodicals Index under "Popular Culture," the subtopic "Fads" produces this entry, among others:

> Anatomy of a fad (torn blue jeans)(Special Edition: The New Teens) by Bill
> Barol il v115 Newsweek Summer–Fall '90 p 40 (2)

Basically, *InfoTrac* is a citation index for periodicals and some books, but it also provides numerous abstracts of articles, and even the full text of some articles. In addition to bibliographic information, you will also be told if the article is available on microfilm and whether your library subscribes to the periodical. As you can see, computerized searches can save you a lot of time and keep you current since files are updated every month.

ProQuest, 1986–
This CD-ROM data base from University Microfilms provides a citation index (with brief abstracts) to over 950 periodicals. By selecting a one-word or two-word subject, the researcher

will be given the number of articles in the database containing the word(s) typed on the screen. If, for example, you were interested in television advertising, you would find an article titled "Spending Grows for Spot, Syndicated TV" in *Advertising Age* for March 8, 1993, that tells you that "ad spending increased 6% from 1991 to nearly $22.8 billion." The citations include a short abstract (this one was 38 words, partially quoted above), which library of a multi-unit library holds it, and whether it is on microform or paper.

Bibliography Cards

As you explore primary and secondary sources, you will need to make a list of potentially useful periodicals and books for your works-cited page. Although there are different ways of listing bibliographical information, using an index card system has the advantage of low-tech versatility: you can sort cards alphabetically without much difficulty and keep the unneeded cards from getting mixed up with the ones you are going to use. Since the cards will eventually be used for the works-cited page, it is a good idea (and strongly recommended) that you put the information into the correct bibliographical form as you do the cards initially. This will save time later on.

Sometimes we'd like to make a demanding job easy—too easy—and we end up wasting time in the long run by saving time in the short run. Let's say that your instructor asks you to turn in twenty bibliography cards. This is one of those cases where you can do a good job or a fast job. Let's concentrate on the former. To begin with, ask yourself three questions:

1. Can you locate what you think is an appropriate source in an index or catalog? Then copy down the essential bibliographic information on a 3x5 card. Go on to the next step.

2. Is the source you've located available? If it is a periodical, does your library have a paper or microform copy? If it is a book, does the library have it available for you to check out? If not, and you think it is an important book for your study, can you get an interlibrary loan? Go on to the next step.

3. Once you possess the periodical or book and you look through it, can you really use it? If yes, you are on the road to completing your study; if no, you've come to a dead end and must go though the process again. But research is frustrating at times, and only a certain percentage of what you think might be useful is actually useful. That's why research is like looking for gold—when you do find it, it's exhilarating, to say nothing of the pot of gold that awaits your disposal!

In summary, it is necessary to evaluate your sources as you go through the research process. Remember the three points above in the following short form:

> Can you find the source?
>
> Can you get the source?
>
> Can you use the source?

Following are six samples of bibliography cards. See Chapter Six, where many more examples of works-cited entries can be found. The information on the examples in Chapter Six is arranged exactly the same way as on the cards that follow.

Bibliography card for a book (fiction). Many libraries will group fictional works according to the last name of the author rather than by a call number. Use the bottom of the card for information that you want to include about the source and then place it in brackets to signify that it is your observation or commentary.

Fiction

O'Connor, Flannery. *The Complete Stories*. New York: Farrar, 1971.

[contains 31 stories]

Bibliography card for a book (non-fiction). Place the call number in the upper left-hand corner in case you return the book to the library and then find that you need to look up something in the book again. This way you will save yourself time by not having to look up the call number on a second occasion.

808.06
  K17r
Kaplan, Robbie Miller. *Resumes, the Write Stuff : A Quick Guide to Presenting Your Qualifications Effectively*. Garrett Park, MD: Garrett Park Press, 1987.
          [bibliography on p. 90]

Bibliography card for a pamphlet. At the top of the card, identify the source as a pamphlet. Note that the author is a committee, the organization is the publisher, and there is no date given for publication. Also, a bracketed note reminds you that "operations research" as a career choice is explained by people who have that job.

Pamphlet

Education Committee. *Careers in Operations Research*. Baltimore: Operations Research Society of America, n.d.
[defines and gives examples of "O.R."]

Figure 3.4   Bibliography Cards (Books and Pamphlet)

Bibliography card for a newspaper. Note that the second author's name is in regular order and that only the first author's name is reversed for alphabetizing purposes on the works-cited page. Also, capitalize every important word of the title of the article, even if the newspaper does not do this in its own headline style.

Bibliography card for a magazine. This is Verlyn Klinkenborg's review of Victoria Glendinning's biographical work on Anthony Trollope (1815–1882), the English novelist. If the book review had a separate title, it would be placed before the title of the book. Also, page numbers are not preceded by "pp." or "pages."

Bibliography card for a journal. Frequently journal titles will be longer to accommodate a concise explanation of the content. The volume number and issue number are separated by a period and precede the year of publication in parentheses. The inclusive page numbers of the article follow the year and are preceded by a colon.

> Hunt, Albert R., and Carla Anne Robbins. "Gephardt Sees Russia Needing Prolonged Aid." <u>Wall Street Journal</u> 13 Apr. 1993, midwest ed. : A3-4.

> Klinkenborg, Verlyn. Rev. of <u>Anthony Trollope</u>, by Victoria Glendinning. <u>Smithsonian</u> Apr. 1993 : 156-59.
>
> [book review]

> Tobin, Gary Allan. "The Bicycle Boom of the 1890's: The Development of Private Transportation and the Birth of the Modern Tourist." <u>Journal of Popular Culture</u> 7.4 (1974) : 838-49.

Figure 3.5 Bibliography Cards (Periodicals)

Exercise 3.1: For a paper you are writing, you have located a book by John W. Smythe called *American Sports in the Nineties*. Published in 1994, the book was a best seller for the Ajax Publishing Company of Cleveland, Tennessee. Write a bibliography card for this book in the space below.

For the same paper, you have located an article from a professional journal called *American Business*. Mary Hopkins and Elizabeth Carpenter co-authored an article called "Computers for Tomorrow" that appeared on pages 66 through 77 of the fourth volume of this journal. Their article came out in issue number three of 1994. Write a bibliography card in the space below.

Chapter 4

The Outline as an Organizing Device

An outline is a logical division of a complex topic into smaller, and therefore more understandable, units. An outline is not an end in itself; it is a writing plan for your paper, a blueprint, a map to where you're going. Like a résumé for a job, an outline shouldn't be too long or long-winded. For a paper of about 1500–2000 words, a page and a half to two pages (double spaced) should provide a thorough topic outline or sentence outline.

The Informal Outline

There are basically two types of outlines—the formal and informal—with variations within each type. The informal outline may consist of a list of ideas in no particular order to begin with and then arranged into a chronological, spatial, or climactic order. The informal outline is a "getting started" outline that is used by the student as a means of clarifying ideas and arranging them in the clearest and most effective way. As you can see from the following example, in this type of outline there is not a great deal of regard for form:

Topic: Professional Sports
Question: Will pro sports maintain their popularity as we head toward the twenty-first century?
Tentative thesis: After fifty years of stasis, modern sports have gone ballistic (kinetic?)
  —Baseball makes an adjustment.
    —Expansion forces new division make-up and playoffs; what's next? purists lament.
    —Will there be any lingering effects from work stoppage? (In football's case, strike was quickly forgotten.)
  —Football expands throughout U.S. and to Europe.
    —World League of American Football (WLAF) exports game to Europe.
    —Satellite transmissions enable international audiences to get acquainted with American game, buy products

—Can football compete with soccer (real "football" to the rest of the world)?

—Will sports merchandise (caps, jerseys, jackets) find favor outside the U.S.?

—Basketball remains a cold-weather favorite.

—"March Madness" catches on. Can college basketball create interest that will carry over to the pro ranks?

—3-point shot rejuvenates the game

—Hockey expansion adds players

—It's not a Canadian game anymore as U.S.-born players join Russians, Czechs, Scandinavians, and others on the ice.

—Olympics create world-wide interest in the sport.

Conclusion: Increasing competition for entertainment dollar will create a dynamic sports agenda for the next ten years.

The outline above is meant to be a working outline. An outline evolves; it isn't written out perfectly just after you start doing your research. As your ideas and opinions become more developed due to the information you've collected and the thought you've put into the topic, so too does the outline become more developed.

The Formal Outline

The formal outline is the one you turn in with your paper. There are two types that are most common: the topic outline and the sentence outline. The formal outline follows the traditional conventions of labeling and indenting according to the importance of the parts of the outline. It would look like this:

Thesis: Since the thesis is the controlling idea of the paper, it's a good idea to place it in a position of prominence to remind you to keep on track.

Introduction: The introduction is in an important position because it is the first thing that greets the reader; make it memorable.

I. **First major division of the topic** In a paper of this size—1,500–2,000 words—it would be best, easiest, and most effective to have between two and five major divisions but not usually more than this because the paper would begin to look choppy and underdeveloped.
   A. **First subdivision**
   B. **Second subdivision** Since an outline is the dividing of a unit, the result of any division must be at least two parts. You can't, for example, cut an orange in half and only have one part. Therefore, if you have an A, you must have a B; you can also have a C, D, E, etc.

II. Second major division This would be another key idea that develops your thesis statement.
- **A. First subdivision**
- **B. Second subdivision**
- **C. Third subdivision**
    - **1. First sub subdivision**
    - **2. Second sub subdivision** Again, remember that if you have a 1, you must have at least a 2 as part of your division.

III. Third major division
- **A. First subdivision**
    - **1. First sub subdivision**
    - **2. Second sub subdivision**
- **B. Second subdivision**
    - **1. First sub subdivision**
    - **2. Second sub subdivision**
    - **3. Third sub subdivision**

Conclusion: Like the Introduction, the Conclusion is in an emphatic position; give your readers something to take with them.

Let's take another look at the outline above but from a different perspective; an "aerial view." In the circular diagram (Figure 4.1), notice how the topic is introduced in a general way that applies to the entire subject; then the thesis statement branches out into three directions

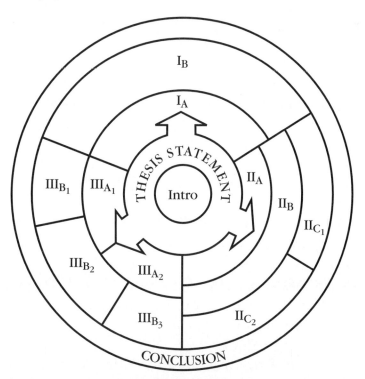

Figure 4.1 Outline Schematic

representing the three major points that will be developed in the paper. The parts that have been further divided represent the components of the subdivisions. The conclusion is represented by a circle that surrounds the entire topic since the conclusion naturally wraps things up and ties everything together.

You can also look at other types of outline configurations: one may look like the branches of a tree, another like the root system of a tree; still another may look like circles connected by straight lines, but whatever the configuration, they all have the same things in common: ideas in a paper are connected to one another. Some ideas are more important than others. Ideas are presented in a certain climactic, spatial, or chronological progression. Outlines, of whatever type, always show relationships between things.

The Topic Outline

Two of the most popular types of formal outlines are the topic outline and the sentence outline. In the topic outline, each unit in the division consists not of complete sentences but of word groups that pinpoint the content of that division. Though a topic outline does not consist of sentences, it should have sufficient words to characterize the thought accurately in each part. Do not, then, use just a word or two in each unit. Here is an example of a topic outline developed from an idea suggested in Chapter One:

Working Title: The Malling of America

Thesis Statement: The growth of the suburban shopping mall signals an automobile-dependent lifestyle that typifies urban alienation and contributes to a lack of community.

Introduction: Will the mall be the herald of the future: an artificial city, a fantasy land of mercantilism, or will it be the core of a stable exurban environment?

  I. Life in the 'burbs, a post-war phenomenon
     A. Cars lead the way out of the cities
     B. Suburbs and their unprecedented growth
     C. Conditions ideal for sprawl
        1. Cheap real estate
        2. Loads of free parking
 II. The auto as prime liberating element in the American lifestyle
     A. Mobility = freedom
     B. Auto sales spur economy
     C. New housing built to accommodate driveway space
     D. People move farther and further apart

III. Malls aren't only alienating factor
    A. Television
    B. Housing
IV. Move toward bigness in American society
    A. Small businesses find it hard to compete
    B. Chain stores and franchises another factor
Conclusion: Retrieve what worked in the past; retain what works today for a healthy synthesis that decreases the distance between Americans.

The Sentence Outline

Unlike the topic outline, the sentence outline is made up of complete sentences in every division of the outline. Since every sentence contains a subject (what or who the sentence is about) and a predicate (what is said about the subject), this type of outline has the advantage of being more complete and more helpful in the process of going from the outline to the rough draft. Either type is acceptable, though of the two, the topic outline is more popular probably because it seems easier to do and is more compact. However, the advantage of the sentence outline should not be overlooked: it forces you to really say something in your outline, and that helps you think better and work more efficiently in the earlier stages of the paper.

    Here is an example of a sentence outline for a paper that deals with John Steinbeck's *The Grapes of Wrath:*

Thesis: John Steinbeck's *The Grapes of Wrath* was an accurate account of the times and social consequences of the Great Depression, and it is historically significant for us today.

Introduction: *The Grapes of Wrath* (both novel and movie) is a mirror of the Great Depression.

I. Steinbeck's accuracy in reporting the conditions in the novel is evaluated.
    A. Steinbeck was not only a writer but an observer.
    B. Steinbeck was educated by the events of the time.
    C. Steinbeck strove to write history in the making.
II. *The Grapes of Wrath* met with mixed reception.
    A. The reception and authenticity of the book were of great concern to Steinbeck.
    B. The reaction of the Associated Farmers campaign was not favorable and was critical of the work.
    C. Farm expert Carey McWilliams defends Steinbeck's depictions.
    D. President Franklin Roosevelt and his wife, Eleanor, commented on the validity of Steinbeck's work.

    E. Three phases of literary criticism brought various responses.
        1. 1940–55: Accuracy and credentials of the author are examined.
        2. 1955–73: Novel's literary values are evaluated.
        3. 1973–89: Biographical and regional fields are investigated.

III. The novel's validity is evaluated by comparing three historical works to Steinbeck's novel.
    A. John Kenneth Galbraith looks at the economic conditions of the Depression.
    B. The accounts of Frederick Lewis Allen and Steinbeck were similar.
        1. Allen's descriptions of the Dust Bowl were similar to Steinbeck's.
        2. The historical analysis of the Dust Bowl was interpreted in the same way by both writers.
    C. Richard Hofstadter shows that the need to solve the problems of the time was confirmed by the policies of President Franklin Roosevelt.

IV. There is a need for social reform today.
    A. Robert Brustein comments on the Broadway play.
    B. Oral historian Studs Terkel says that there are modern parallels to the Joads of the 1930s.

Conclusion: Steinbeck's novel reflects the economic, social, and political plight of the Okies during the Depression and provides the reader with insights into the continual need for reform to create a better life for the "underprivileged" in the 1930s as well as today.

A Half-Dozen Outline Reminders

- Remember that an outline is a working plan and that it will develop as you go along. Don't expect too much at first, but the more information you collect and the more knowledge about the topic you attain, the easier the research process becomes.

- An outline shows relationships between things; that is its essential function. An outline is not a random arrangement of items.

- An outline is a logical division of a topic; therefore, if you have an A, you must have a B; if you have a 1, you must have a 2, etc.

- Outlines should change; be prepared to add, delete, and rearrange.

- Choose concise nouns and verbs (especially verbs) for your outline.

- A good thesis statement is the heart of the outline.

Chapter 5

Taking Notes: Using Other People's Ideas and Information

Knowing what notes to take and how to take them is at the heart of the research process. Simply put, if you don't take good notes, you won't write a good research paper. Your reading and notes provide the evidence to support your analysis, evaluation, and argument. There are different ways of taking notes and different formats to put them in. Let's take a look at five types:

The Direct Quotation

Sometimes you need to use the exact words of a source (at least in the initial stages of your research) especially when the quotation is well stated, possesses interesting sound qualities because of alliteration or onomatopoeia, for example, or because the quotation is humorous, controversial, or even wrong-headed. But don't overuse direct quotation because the reader wants to hear your voice, not everyone else's. Why? It helps the reader focus on one person's ideas—yours!

> **Thoreau 175**   **Thoreau's Observations on the News**
>
> *"And I am sure that I never read any memorable news in a newspaper. If we read of one man robbed, or murdered, or killed by accident, or one house burned, or one vessel wrecked, or one steamboat blown up, or one cow run over on the Western Railroad, or one mad dog killed, or one lot of grasshoppers in the winter—we never need read of another. One is enough. If you are acquainted with the principle, what do you care for a myriad instances and applications? To a philosopher all news, as it is called, is gossip...."*

In the above example from Henry David Thoreau's *Walden,* the author's last name is placed at the top of the card along with the page number(s) of the quotation. To the right is a "slug," which the *Random House College Dictionary* defines as "a short phrase or title used [by journalists] to indicate the content of copy. Make sure you put quotation marks before and after the quoted material. Any interpolations (comments or explanations about the quoted material by you) are put in brackets. Use spaced ellipsis periods (. . .) to indicate any words removed from the original. (Remember: any time you take words out, make sure that what remains makes sense, and, if necessary, insert the correct punctuation at the elliptical break if you've changed the sentence structure from complex to compound, for example; this change might require that a semicolon or comma and coordinating conjunction be inserted within brackets to prevent misreading or to avoid a comma splice.)

The preceding format is good for relatively short direct quotations; for long ones it may be better to photocopy the page(s) from the original source and then use a highlighter to mark important ideas. (Otherwise, you'll be spending a lot of time just copying out information verbatim.) Use the margins for your comments; use the top of the page for the author, page numbers, and a slug.

The Regular Paraphrase

In a paraphrase, the researcher borrows the ideas of another person and puts those ideas into his or her own words and own style of writing. A paraphrase is roughly the same length as the original, but the sentence structure should be the researcher's own, not the original author's. Moreover, paraphrasing doesn't mean changing a word here and there or merely substituting synonyms; paraphrasing is not a word-for-word translation. Rather, paraphrasing is taking an idea, an abstraction, and making it concrete with your words, your style, and your voice (if an English person explained to you how a mulching mower worked, you would not explain the process to someone else using a British accent!).

Here is a paraphrase of the Thoreau quotation above:

> *Thoreau 175   Thoreau and the News*
>
> *[One wonders what Thoreau would say about local television news since he comes down pretty hard on the pre-electronic news media of the 1850s.] Commenting on people's penchant for the news, Henry David Thoreau says that he can't remember ever reading anything really worthwhile in a newspaper. He feels that if we are aware of what's going on in our environment, we needn't constantly reaffirm what we already know: that people are sometimes victimized by crime, that they have accidents, that their houses burn down, that ships sink, that cows get killed when they wander onto railroad tracks, that rabid dogs get despatched because of their threat to society, and that even something as unusual as a swarm of grasshoppers during the winter might occur. In short, though we know that disaster strikes, that unpleasant things do occur, being greedy for these things in the newspaper won't make them go away nor make us better people.*

The bracketed first sentence in the above example is the researcher's lead-in to the paraphrase. It will make transferring the note to the rough draft less difficult since the transition is already there. Also, to make your job easier and to save time later, introduce your paraphrase with the source's name (use the first and last name the first time you cite the person; every time thereafter use just the last name). Also, as with the direct quotation, at the top of the card, use the source's last name, page number(s), and a slug.

The Summary Paraphrase

The summary is also a paraphrase, but it is a paraphrase of only the gist of an idea; it concentrates on the main items but leaves out many of the details that we would ordinarily find in a regular paraphrase. It is, therefore, shorter than a regular paraphrase. Here, for example, is a summary of the Thoreau passage above:

> ### Thoreau 175   Thoreau and the News
>
> *Referring to murders, robberies, fires, explosions, Thoreau says that once you have read about one of these and understand what it means, then you need not keep reading about them since repetition is not going to enhance your understanding.*

Combining Paraphrase and Direct Quotation

Since long quotations of five lines or more break up a page and since too many long quotations are distracting (and maybe even a bit old-fashioned) and since integrating short quotations into your discussion smoothly makes for easier reading, the combination of paraphrase and direct quotation is one of the best ways of recording the ideas of others.

In the following two paragraphs by Horace P. Beck ["Where the Workers of the World Unite." *Our Living Traditions: An Introduction to Folklore*. Ed. Tristram Potter Coffin. New York: Basic, 1968, 58–59.], we have a good description of folkloric heroes. In the blocked material following, the use of direct quotation and paraphrase combines to consolidate the note and highlight important phrasing from the original.

Nearly every occupation seems to have a folk hero. Among the better known are the sailor's Old Stormalong; the river boatman's Mike Fink; the cowboy's Pecos Bill; the midwestern farmer's Febold Feboldson; the steel worker's Joe Magarac; the lumberman's Paul Bunyan; and the railroader's John Henry and Casey Jones.

All of these heroes are, in large measure, comic characters.... All of them, with the possible exception of Casey Jones, are giants, and all are benevolent. Their activities are usually bumbling but beneficial. The good they do is most often accidental and is usually attended by an unexpected calamity which the giant is forced to rectify with as much or more difficulty than he encountered in his initial effort. Often the giants are accompanied by a small helper, who, although feeble in physical powers, is titanic in mental ability. The small one's brains complement the muscular prowess of his huge friend.

Beck 58–59   *Occupational Heroes Defined*

Since workers spend nearly one-third of their lives at their jobs, it seems fitting that occupations have their own heroes. As Horace P. Beck tells us, most occupational heroes are good-natured giants who stumble comically through a series of misadventures to accomplish some good for humankind. As Beck puts it, "their activities are bumbling but beneficial." To make up for the giants' inadequate brain power and to help them out of the mess they created, their authors provide them with sidekicks, "feeble in physical powers, [but] titanic in mental ability." Together, they make a good example of a folkloric odd couple.

In the method illustrated above, as in the others, place the author's last name, page number(s), and slug prominently at the top of the card. Notice also the necessary use of bracketed material to make the sentence read correctly.

Your Own Notes

It is important to take note of your own ideas and observations, your reactions to what critics say, your synthesis of materials, your conclusions, and so on. You do this for three reasons: (1) so you don't forget a good idea of yours, (2) so your paper is not all other people's ideas, opinions, observations, etc., and (3) because the reader really wants to know what you think about things since this is your paper, not somebody else's.

An example of the kind of personal note mentioned above follows in the next block:

> ### My Ideas on Occupational Heroes
>
> *It wouldn't work if the scenario were reversed: if the giants were the smart guys and the sidekicks were the ones who were the stumblebums, but it might make for an interesting alternative to the standard stories! Why do folkloric stories seem to take a certain pattern? Do people like the same stories over and over again with slight modifications? Perhaps; take a look at the similarities that we find on TV shows, where there is not too much departure from something that apparently works ... and makes a lot of money!*

The above note is in conversational form because it contains ideas generated quickly and put down quickly, before they are forgotten. Later, you can polish up the note. Try to make it a habit to include your observations on the topic in note form to ensure that your voice is heard in the paper. Here is another example, this time the compilation of statistical data gleaned from merely observing what has been written on a certain topic:

> ### My Primary Observations on TQM
>
> *There is no scarcity of periodical articles written on Total Quality Management. In the period from 1986 to November 1993, there were 599 entries in the InfoTrac listings under 48 categories ranging from "Accounting and auditing" to "Usage."*

Color-Coding Tips for Notes and Rough Draft

To make life easier as a researcher, develop ways of doing things that are more efficient. Using different colored markers on your cards to indicate major divisions of your outline or certain kinds of material (definitions, etc.) can speed up identification of a card because all you have to do is locate a color rather than root through a stack of cards every time you need to look something up. Also, indicating direct quotations on a rough draft with a certain color will let you know at a glance if there is too much quotation and not enough of your voice in your paper. Also, putting colored brackets before and after paraphrased materials on the rough draft will let you (and your instructor) know how you are handling your borrowed information and opinions.

What Is Plagiarism?

Plagiarism is defined as using someone else's words or ideas without acknowledging the source. (Curiously, the root of this word means to "kidnap" or "plunder.") We can divide plagiarism into two types: intentional and unintentional. Flagrant *intentional* plagiarism usually results in an F grade (or worse). Examples of intentional plagiarism include copying someone else's research paper and turning it in under your own name; buying a research paper from a private or commercial source; copying out paragraphs (even sentences) of articles or books and incorporating them into your paper without documentation; lifting ideas or interpretations from other sources without acknowledgment; and using the syntax (sentence structure) from other sources in paraphrases (with or without documentation, this is not permitted).

Unintentional plagiarism occurs because of ignorance or carelessness. In either case, it will lower your grade if it is frequent or extensive. If you forget to put quotation marks around a sentence but document it, that would technically be plagiarism, but in reality it is more the result of carelessness and the lack of careful proofreading, and you might lose points for that lapse. It should also be noted that ignorance is not much of a defense for plagiarism because the student should be familiar with the methodology of research and its protocols.

Do You Have to Document Everything?

No. *Common knowledge,* or "public domain," information does not have to be documented. What is common knowledge? Facts and statistics readily available in many reference sources would be an example. Here are some specific instances that would qualify: the list of people who served on the Warren Commission; the speed of sound at sea level; the year of presidential appointment (and by whom) and political party of Supreme Court Justices; the size of a soccer field; the deepest part of the Pacific ocean; the year Ted Williams batted .406 (or any sports statistic); the commonly stated causes of the Civil War. In fact, the more you read about a topic, you will find that many things qualify as common knowledge that you did not realize before. For example, when you read the literary critics of Flannery O'Connor's short stories, they will point out that she frequently uses the sun as a symbol. When you read "Greenleaf," sure enough, there is the sun as a symbol of energy and power, among other things. As a rule of thumb, if at least three sources say essentially (not approximately, but essentially) the same thing, that would probably qualify as common knowledge. Now let's take a look at what is not common knowledge.

Anything that is debatable, unique, subject to refutation, is one person's opinion rather than fact, or anything that has been superseded by new knowledge and is therefore somewhat controversial (like the remeasurement of a mountain with different results from the commonly held figures in reference books) has to be documented. Also, paraphrased common knowledge items have to be documented, but individual extrapolations from common-knowledge reference sources need not be documented since there is not extensive reliance on the borrowed source.

Should You Document Even Though You Don't Have to?

Sure, sometimes. You document for a number of reasons: (1) to give credit to the source (it's a kind of non-monetary royalty you pay for the use of that person's knowledge, scholarship, and ideas); (2) to show the reader that you didn't simply make something up, that you can point to a source; and (3) to emphasize the location where somebody can find the information that you are referring to. So, to be helpful to the reader, you might very well provide the source for information that would be considered common knowledge.

Guidelines for Using Paraphrases and Direct Quotations

- Be faithful to the source; don't make Marie Winn, for example, say things that she didn't say in her book. Remember: you are putting her ideas into your words.

- Integrate the note into your rough draft smoothly. The easiest way to ensure proper flow is to write your note with your rough draft in mind. Provide a lead-in, when necessary, for coherence.

- Don't quote only one word, as a rule, unless you are placing special emphasis on that single word. You would usually use quotation marks for two or more consecutive words.

- Quote memorable phrases or sentences, like "bumbling but beneficial," but not ordinary phrases or sentences, like "the giants are accompanied by a small helper."

- When paraphrasing, must you in all cases avoid words used by the source unless you quote them directly? No, sometimes you have to use the same words (what could you substitute for giant?—large person?!), but don't overdo it.

Exercise 5.1: Which of the following would have to be documented and why?

1. The number of Baptist churches in the United States
2. The date of the first "talking" movie
3. Comments about *The Grapes of Wrath* in John Steinbeck's *Letters*
4. The number of miles in a light year
5. Christopher Columbus's egg trick

Exercise 5.2: Comment on the two different versions of the paragraph from Juliet B. Schor's book *The Overworked American: The Unexpected Decline of Leisure*. New York: Basic, 1991. The original text is below, followed by two paraphrases:

In the last twenty years the amount of time Americans have spent at their jobs has risen steadily. Each year the change is small, amounting to about nine hours, or slightly more than one additional day of work. In any given year, such a small increment has probably been imperceptible. But the accumulated increase over two decades is substantial. When surveyed, Americans report that they have only

Author Mentioned in Text

In this next example, since the directly quoted material is fewer than five lines, incorporate it into the paragraph. Since the author's name is mentioned in the introduction, you do not have to put it within the parentheses with the page number:

> John Steinbeck uses the rhetorical figure called epistrophe when he repeats the phrase "I'll be there" in Tom Joad's famous speech in The Grapes of Wrath (537).

Whole Book Being Cited (No Page Number Given)

If you are citing a whole book, you will not need to give a page number in parentheses since you are not referring to any one page in particular. The following is an example of such a citation:

> Henry Petroski, a professor of civil engineering at Duke University, delves into the area of industrial design in his book The Evolution of Useful Things. Fresh from the success of his previous work, The Pencil, Petroski now tackles the paper clip, the four-tined fork, the zipper, the pop-top aluminum can, McDonald's polystyrene-foam clamshell containers (discontinued for environmental reasons in 1990), and other artifacts from commercial America, like Post-it notes, the Bostitch stapler, and plastic garbage bags.

Two Authors

List both authors in the text or in the parenthetical citation, but do not do both:

> William Strunk, Jr., and E.B. White, authors of one of the best and briefest books on effective writing, The Elements of Style, stress the importance of creating word pictures: "If those who have studied the art of writing are in accord on any one point, it is on this: the surest way to arouse and hold the attention of the reader is by being specific, definite, and concrete" (21).

Three Authors

If the authors' names are not mentioned in the text, then list them in the parenthetical citation:

> The world bird population has been estimated at 100 billion (Robbins, Bruun, and Zim 6).

Four or More Authors

With four or more authors, simply list the first one followed by "et al." ("and others"):

> It is estimated that between 70 and 90 percent of the words we customarily use are Anglo-Saxon (Hodges et al. 206).

Corporate Authorship

Sometimes a book or article will be written by a committee; therefore, list the organization that produced the work (it may be the same as the publisher in some instances):

> The Warren Commission concluded that "two bullets probably caused all the wounds suffered by President Kennedy and Governor Connally" (President's Commission 117). [The "Warren Commission" is the informal name of the President's Commission on the Assassination of President John F. Kennedy.]

No Author Credited

In older magazines and for short pieces in periodicals, articles sometimes appear without attribution. When this occurs, the title (or a shortened version of a long title) precedes the page number:

> Since 1991, there have been 50 percent more mentions of Elvis sightings in the New York Times ("Harper's Index" 11).

Two Works by the Same Author

Let's say that you are using two David Feldman books, *Do Penguins Have Knees?* and *Why Do Clocks Run Clockwise?*, in your works cited. When you have a parenthetical citation, list a shortened version of the title before the page number:

> David Feldman takes up the perplexing question "How do they decide where to put thumbnotches in dictionaries?" (Penguins 167–68).

Multivolume Work

If your works-cited entry lists a work of several volumes, your parenthetical citation within the text should list the specific volume before the page number:

> Joseph Conrad creates interesting effects with point of view: "The use of intermediate narrators and multiple points of view is common in Conrad; it is his favorite way of suggesting the complexity of experience and the difficulty of judging human actions" (Abrams et al. 2: 1497).

Tertiary Source

It is not a good idea to use too many thirdhand sources, but sometimes it is necessary. In order to indicate the borrowing clearly and to avoid confusion as to where the source appears, use "qtd. in" before the name and page of the source in which the author is found:

> The "not-but" construction, also known as antithesis, is illustrated by Shakespeare's "Not that I loved Caesar less, but that I loved Rome more" (qtd. in Booth and Gregory 114).

Poetry Quotations

Short poetry quotations (one or two lines) should be integrated into the paragraph and set off by quotation marks. Use a virgule (slash mark) after the last word or mark of punctuation of the first line and continue the second line immediately following the virgule. Here is a two-line example:

> Alfred, Lord Tennyson's "Ulysses," a poem about the mythical Greek hero Odysseus (Ulysses in Latin), contains the following advice for his Victorian audience: "How dull it is to pause, to make and end,/ To rust unburnished, not to shine in use" (22–23).

Extended poetry quotations (three or more lines) should be set off by indenting ten spaces from the left margin. Since indention substitutes for quotation marks, do not use them unless they appear in the original, in which case reproduce them exactly as they appear. In the example that follows, note that the original look of the poem is maintained by the spacing preceding each line:

> In "Binsey Poplars," a poem written in 1879, Gerard Manley Hopkins laments the effects of the destruction of trees on both the botanical environment and the human environment:
>
>> O if we but knew what we do
>>> When we delve or hew—
>> Hack and rack the growing green! (9–11)

The following extended poetry example is from a drama, poetic segments of which are set off, as above, by indenting ten spaces from the left:

> Polonius concludes his advice to his son, Laertes, with these famous six lines:
>
>> Neither a borrower nor a lender be;
>> For loan oft loses both itself and friend,
>> And borrowing dulls the edge of husbandry.
>> This above all: to thine own self be true,
>> And it must follow, as the night the day,
>> Thou canst not then be false to any man.
>>> (Hamlet 1.3.75–80)

In the poetry quotations above, note that the selection cited is indicated within parentheses. If the poem or play is not mentioned before the lines are quoted, then indicate the name of the poem or play before the line numbers and enclose all of this information within parentheses, as in the *Hamlet* notation above.

Introduce Your Quotations and Paraphrases

For a paraphrase or direct quotation, introduce the originator of the borrowed material (author, committee, company, organization, wire service, government body, etc.) at the beginning. For an individual, use the person's full name; thereafter use only the last name. With an organization, use the full name first (National Aeronautics and Space Administration); then use the familiar abbreviation (NASA) thereafter. Just as you would give some background about a person you are introducing to someone else, so too give some background about the authority you are quoting. This adds coherence to your writing and makes it more interesting. Ultimately, the reader wants to know whom you are citing, where this information comes from, and why you are citing that source. Therefore, for first references, it may be better to provide that information in the text rather than in a sparse parenthetical reference at the end. In the following example (Oxford: Oxford UP, 1992), note how the introduction puts the quoted matter into perspective:

> In his introduction to the Oxford Book of the Sea, Jonathan Raban writes of the beautiful but foreboding sea, how it captivates our psyche and influences our language:
>
>> Modern English is littered with dead nautical metaphors like aloof [literally, sailing toward the wind], which were alive and well when Shakespeare was writing. To have things above board . . . to be taken aback . . . to see something out to the bitter end (the last extremity of the anchor-chain, where it is attached to the bitt, and a sure sign of desperate circumstances)—the most landlubberly speaker of colloquial English is prone to talk unconsciously in terms that come out of the sea. (7)

In addition to the foregoing, there are other ways to introduce information so as to let the reader know who is the originator of the sentences on the page. (Remember that the reader will assume that you are the source of all the words on the page unless you let the reader know otherwise.) Here are some of them:

- Use a noun substitute for the person or organization: "A psychologist studying the effects of television on behavior explained the difficulties encountered in the experiment . . ."

- Announce a lengthy or complicated example beforehand: "Architects for the new stadium listed all the state-of-the-art features that would be crowd pleasers . . ."

- The first sentence of a new paragraph indicates the beginning of a new idea. If the first sentence ends with a page reference, the reader obviously knows that the sentence contains the referenced borrowed material, and no formal introduction is needed in this case.

- If there is any confusion as to who is talking in the paper, make sure you clarify who is speaking: you or someone else.

Exercise 6.1: In the space provided below or on a separate sheet of paper, write an introduction from your reading that provides background information about the source, perhaps where the information comes from, and why it is important. Here is an example from *TQManager: A Practical Guide for Managing in a Total Quality Organization.* Jossey-Bass Management Ser. San Francisco: Jossey-Bass, 1993:

> In their latest book on Total Quality Management, Warren H. Schmidt, a professor emeritus in public administration at the University of Southern California, and Jerome P. Finnigan, an executive with Xerox, call the quality movement "the most significant shift in American management thought and practice since the Industrial Revolution a century ago" (xii).

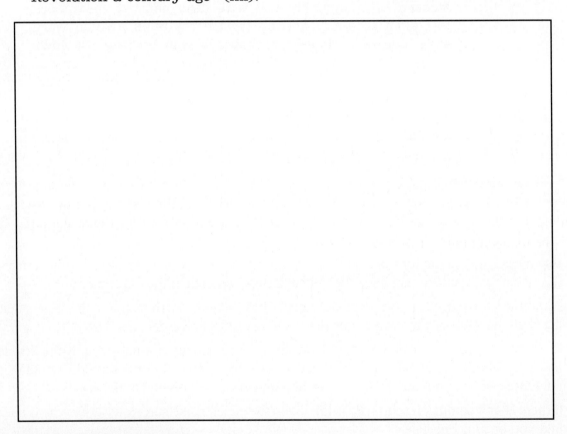

The Works-Cited Entry

The word "cited" means "shown" or "listed" or "referred to"; thus, any work that you have referred to in the text of your paper you will list on a separate sheet at the end of your paper. But you will not list works that you only consulted but did not refer to. Only those works that appear in black and white in your paper will appear on the list of "Works Cited" at the end of your paper.

The following four general formats for works-cited entries will be followed by specific examples, but the general formats are listed for your convenience and easy reference:

General Format for a Book

Use the numbered elements in the sample entry that apply to the book you are citing:

```
      1                    2                      3
Author. "Chapter or Part of a Book." Title of Book:
               4              5        6                    7
      Subtitle. Ed. [Name]. 2nd ed. 2 vols. Series [Name and number].
           8         9          10        11                  12
      City: Publisher, Year. Pages used. Supplementary Information.
```

1: Give the author's last name first, followed by the first name and middle initial, unless the author prefers otherwise: Baum, L. Frank; Millay, Edna St. Vincent; Milne, A.A. If you happen to be quoting or paraphrasing the editor or translator of a work, then his or her name goes in this position followed by "ed." or "trans." [Browne, Ray B., ed.]

2: List the "chapter" only if it is singularly important to your study; use "part of a book" for a short story, poem, play, essay, etc. that appears in an anthology.

3: Underline the title of the book and the subtitle; subtitles are found mostly in academic books and further define the purpose of the book; the subtitle is preceded by a colon unless the main title ends in a question mark, exclamation point, or a dash.

4: The editor of a collection of poems, plays, short stories, essays, etc. goes here when the editor is not the one quoted or paraphrased. The editor's name is given in regular order; the last name comes first only if it appears as the first item in an entry. [Ed. Ray B. Browne] (A translator or compiler is treated in the same way as an editor.)

5: The edition number is given only if it is a revised, second or later edition. It is abbreviated in the following manner: 2nd ed., 3rd ed., 4th ed., etc.

6: List the total volumes for that particular work (2 vols.); if you concentrated on only one of the volumes, however, just list that one (Vol. 2.).

7: If a book is part of a series, list the name and the number of that work in the series: University of Minnesota Pamphlets on American Writers 54.

8: If several cities are listed on the title page, just list the first one since that is usually the main office of the publishing company. List the state only if the reader might not know where the city is located or if there are two comparably sized cities with the same name.

9: Use a shortened version of the publisher's name; do not include "Co." or "Inc." [Use just Norton; not W.W. Norton and Co., Inc.]

10: Use the latest copyright date on the title page for the date of publication. Do not confuse copyright with printing history.

11: List inclusive pages only if you listed a chapter from a book or a short story, poem, play, etc. from a collection; otherwise, listing pages is unnecessary since the whole book is being cited.

12: If necessary, any additional information or annotation goes here.

General Format for a Newspaper

Use the numbered elements that apply to the newspaper you are citing:

  1   **2**   **3**   **4**

Author. "Title of Article." <u>Name of Newspaper</u> [City]
      5   **6**   **7**
  Day Month Year [Edition]: Inclusive page numbers.

1: Give the author's last name first, followed by the first name and middle initial, unless the author prefers otherwise: Royko, Mike; Quinn, Jane Bryant; Tolkien, J.R.R. In newspapers as well as magazines, there is a possibility for anonymous or unsigned articles, especially in older periodicals. If this is the case, begin the works-cited entry with the title of the article.

2: The title of the article is enclosed within quotation marks and followed by a period. In some instances, you might cite a letter to the editor, an editorial, an editorial cartoon, a chart or graph, etc. In this case you identify what you have borrowed (Letter), but do not put it within quotation marks because you are identifying it rather than giving an actual title. In the case of an editorial give both the descriptive title (Editorial) preceded by the title of the editorial ("Clean Air a Priority").

3: Underline the name of the newspaper: <u>New York Times</u>. You need not provide the definite article *The* before the newspaper name.

4: If the name does not include the city, then supply the city name within brackets following the name of the newspaper: <u>Plain Dealer</u> [Cleveland]. If you need to add the state after the city, use the two-letter postal abbreviations: <u>Times-Leader</u> [Wilkes-Barre, PA].

5: List the day, month, and year for the newspaper: 4 Mar. 1993. As with magazines, do not indicate a volume number even if the newspaper lists one in its masthead. Newspapers are put on microfilm; they are not bound into volumes. Abbreviate all months except May, June, and July.

6: If you can determine what edition the paper is, indicate this information between the date and the page number of the article: city ed., state ed., midwest ed., natl ed.

7: List the inclusive page numbers for the article: A6–7. As with the magazine, if the article is lengthy and jumps from page to page, just give the beginning page followed by a plus: A4+, but if the article is contained on two non-successive pages, give both: A4, A12. Note that some newspapers paginate differently: by section number followed by page numbers (sec. 5: 1, 5), by letters followed by page numbers (A1, A5), or without divisions and by continuous pagination (34–35).

General Format for a Magazine

Use the numbered elements that apply to the magazine you are citing:

```
      1                2                      3               4
Author. "Title of Article." Name of Magazine Day Month
                            5
        Year: Inclusive page numbers.
```

1: Give the author's last name first, followed by the first name and middle initial, unless the author prefers otherwise: Baker, Russell; Huffam, Charles John; Rosenthal A.M. In a magazine as well as a newspaper, there is the possibility for anonymous or unsigned articles, especially in older periodicals. If that is the case, begin your works-cited entry with the title of the article.

2: The title of the article will be enclosed in quotation marks; capitalize all the words with the exception of small function words like "the," "in," "over," "of," etc.

3: The name of the magazine should be underlined. At this point you may be wondering what the difference is between a magazine and a journal. Let's compare the two and note the differences: a journal is usually published by a learned society or professional organization to disseminate information and opinion about the subject matter of interest to that group (literature, medicine, petroleum engineering, etc.). Since magazines are published as commercial ventures, they will try to attract a large readership and sell enough advertising to generate a profit. Journals will have a small circulation, contain long articles with documentation, will have little or no advertising, be published usually without many pictures, be printed on heavier paper, and are meant to be saved. Magazines, on the other hand, are colorful and graphically appealing, will contain rather short articles without footnotes or bibliography, and are intended to be read quickly and then discarded, to be replaced by next week's or next month's issue.

4: Since libraries do not usually send a year's worth of magazines to the bindery to be bound in hard cover and placed on the shelves as a volume, we do not need to specify the volume number (even though the magazine will list one). Instead, list the day for a weekly, followed by the month and year of that issue (20 Feb. 1993). For a monthly magazine, list the month and year without a comma between them (Feb. 1993). Abbreviate all months except May, June, and July.

5: Provide inclusive page numbers for the article: 34–39. If, however, the article begins on page 34, jumps to page 38, then is continued on pages 45–46, and then finally page 54, you can simplify this by placing a plus sign [+] after the first page number [34+], indicating that the article begins on that page but is continued on different pages throughout the magazine.

General Format for a Scholarly or Professional Journal

Use the numbered elements that apply to the journal you are citing:

```
     1                    2                        3
Author. "Title of Article." Name of Journal
              4            5            6                    7
     Series number Volume number (Date): Inclusive page numbers.
```

1: Give the author's last name first, followed by the first name and middle initial, unless the author prefers otherwise: Wilson, John Dover; Eliot, T.S.; cummings, e.e.

2: Set off the title with quotation marks and, as for all titles, capitalize the first and last word and every important word in the title.

3: The name of the journal is underlined and sometimes is known by initials (Publications of the Modern Language Association is simplified to PMLA) instead of a long, full name. If you are unsure, take a look at the publication itself and see how it is referred to in its pages.

4: Use a series number only if a journal began a new series (ns) with a new numbering system after, perhaps, the journal ceased publication for a time and then began anew. The old series (os) would then refer to those volumes prior to the institution of a new numbering system.

5: The volume number for a journal is given in Arabic numerals; the issue number (needed for separately paginated issues) is also in Arabic numerals and is preceded by a period with no intervening space: 6.2. When you compare a journal to a magazine you will note that you need not list the volume number for a magazine, and you may wonder why that is. Let's take a step back to consider what a volume is. The word *volvere* means "to turn," and a volume originally was a scroll, a rolled-up piece of parchment or other material, that made up a unit. Libraries gather together all the issues that make up a volume and send them to a book binder to have a hard cover put on them; all the issues taken together in this way then constitute a unit and are accorded a volume number for each unit. Since magazines have many more issues per volume, and since magazines are printed on less durable paper and are not meant to be saved, libraries put issues of magazines on microfilm and preserve them that way rather than in bound volume form.

6: For a journal, the year is sufficient since you already know the volume number. If the pagination is continuous throughout the volume and if the volume covers two years, then give both years as the date: 1990–91. If a journal is paged anew for each issue, then it is important that you give both volume and issue number: 6.2.

7: Provide inclusive page numbers for the start and finish of the article: 177–89. Unlike magazines, journals do not usually "jump" pages from one section to another and so pages are consecutive rather than scattered throughout the periodical.

Works-Cited Entries for Books

(Included in these listings are works mentioned in this text.)

Single Author

Feldman, David. <u>Do Penguins Have Knees? An Imponder-
    ables Book</u>. New York: Harper Perennial-Harper,
    1991.

The first line is flush left; second and succeeding lines are indented five spaces. (This is called a hanging indent.)

---. <u>When Did Wild Poodles Roam the Earth? An Imponder-
    ables Book</u>. New York: Harper, 1992.

For two or more works by the same author, use three hyphens as a substitute for the author's name.

Medved, Michael. <u>Hollywood Vs. America: Popular Culture
    and the War on Traditional Values</u>. New York:
    Harper-Zondervan, 1992.

Two publishers are listed because this is a joint publishing venture.

Petroski, Henry. <u>The Evolution of Useful Things</u>. New
    York: Knopf, 1992.

Schor, Juliet B. <u>The Overworked American: The Unex-
    pected Decline of Leisure</u>. New York: Basic, 1991.

Steinbeck, John. <u>The Grapes of Wrath</u>. 1939. New York:
    Penguin, 1976.

For a reprinted book, place the original year of publication after the title and the year of the reprint after the publisher's name.

Two Authors

Booth, Wayne, and Marshall W. Gregory. <u>The Harper & Row
    Rhetoric: Writing as Thinking / Thinking as Writ-
    ing</u>. New York: Harper, 1987.

Note that the second author's name is in regular order; only the first author's last name comes first for purposes of alphabetizing a list of works cited.

Strunk, William, Jr., and E. B. White. <u>The Elements of
    Style</u>. 3rd ed. New York: Macmillan, 1979.

Note where *Jr.* is placed and set it off with a comma before and after.

Three Authors

Robbins, Chandler S., Bertel Bruun, and Herbert S. Zim.
    <u>Birds of North America: A Guide to Field Identifi-
    cation</u>. New York: Golden, 1966.

Four or More Authors

Hodges, John C., et al. <u>Harbrace College Handbook</u>. 11th
    ed. San Diego: Harcourt, 1990.

You may write out all the authors' names, or you may indicate the first author's name and then append "et al." after it to indicate that there are at least three more authors of this work.

Corporate Author

President's Commission. <u>Report of the President's Com-
    mission on the Assassination of President John F.
    Kennedy</u>. 1964. Stamford, CT: Longmeadow, 1992.

Chapter or Part of a Book

Beck, Horace P. "Where the Workers of the World Unite."
    <u>Our Living Traditions: An Introduction to
    Folklore</u>. Ed. Tristram Potter Coffin. New York:
    Basic, 1968. 58-69.

When you cite a complete portion of a book, give the inclusive page numbers of that part of the book.

Short Story, Play, Poem, Essay in a Collection

Weidman, Jerome. "My Father Sits in the Dark." <u>Jewish-
    American Stories</u>. Ed. Irving Howe. New York: Men-
    tor-NAL, 1977. 118-21.

Note that this format is exactly the same as the preceding entry because it too is part of a book. Note also that "Mentor" is the New American Library's imprint for one of its books and is included in the publisher's section and is followed by a hyphen that connects it to the parent company.

Poe, Edgar Allan. "The Cask of Amontillado." <u>The Works
    of Edgar Allan Poe.</u> Vol. 1. N.p. Lippincott, 1895.
    Online. Wiretap. Internet. 21 Mar. 1995.

After the regular book entry, add the delivery medium [Online], the electronic source of the material [Internet Wiretap Online Library was shortened to Wiretap to avoid duplication of words], the computer network [Internet], and the date of access [21 Mar. 1995].

Subtitle

Panati, Charles. <u>Panati's Parade of Fads, Follies, and</u>
    <u>Manias: The Origins of Our Most Cherished Obses-</u>
    <u>sions</u>. New York: Harper Perennial-Harper, 1991.

Subtitles give additional information about the book's contents. Subtitles are preceded by a colon unless the main title ends with a question mark, dash, or exclamation point.

Editor (Author Cited)

Milton, John. <u>Complete Poems and Major Prose</u>. Ed. Mer-
    ritt Y. Hughes. New York: Odyssey, 1957.

Use this form when you are quoting, paraphrasing, or summarizing the author of the book.

Editor (Editor Cited)

Hughes, Merritt Y., ed. <u>Complete Poems and Major Prose</u>.
    By John Milton. New York: Odyssey, 1957.

Use this form when you are quoting, paraphrasing, or summarizing what the editor is saying as in a note or commentary. Note also that the author's name appears after the title and is preceded with the word "By." In addition, this form is also used for a translator or compiler of a work; simply substitute "Trans." or "Comp." for "Ed." It is also possible for one person to do two or all of these functions; if this is the case, write "Trans. and Ed." etc.

Edition Number (2nd ed. and Up)

Perrine, Laurence, and Thomas R. Arp. <u>Sound and Sense:</u>
    <u>An Introduction to Poetry</u>. 8th ed. Fort Worth:
    Harcourt, 1992.

Volumes

Abrams, M.H., et al., eds. <u>The Norton Anthology of Eng-</u>
    <u>lish Literature</u>. Rev. ed. 2 vols. New York: Nor-
    ton, 1968.

Note that a second edition is sometimes called a revised edition. If only one of the two volumes is used and cited, then use the following format that specifies the individual volume:

Abrams, M.H., et al., eds. <u>The Norton Anthology of Eng-</u>
    <u>lish Literature</u>. Rev. ed. Vol. 2. New York: Nor-
    ton, 1968.

Book in a Series

Hyman, Stanley Edgar. <u>Flannery O'Connor</u>. University of
    Minnesota Pamphlets on American Writers 54. Min-
    neapolis: U of Minnesota P, 1966.

Abbreviate "University" and "Press" with single letters not followed by a period.

Supplementary Information after Entry

Chaucer, Geoffrey. <u>The Works of Geoffrey Chaucer</u>. 2nd
    ed. Ed. F.N. Robinson. Boston: Houghton, 1957.
    Contains extensive explanatory notes and glossary.

Stewart, J.I.M. <u>Eight Modern Writers</u>. Oxford: Oxford
    UP, 1963. The eight writers are Hardy, James,
    Shaw, Conrad, Kipling, Yeats, Joyce, and Lawrence.

Reprint

Shelley, Mary. <u>Frankenstein</u>. 1818. New York: Bantam,
    1981.

This is a Bantam paperback reprint of a work originally published in 1818. The original publishing
date immediately follows the title.

Publisher's Imprint

Swift, Jonathan. <u>Gulliver's Travels</u>. 1726. New York:
    Signet-NAL, 1983.

The New American Library, a subsidiary of Penguin Books, has a number of special imprints: in addition to Signet, NAL also publishes Mentor, Onyx, Plume, Meridian, and NAL books. Also note that
the original date is once again given for this reprint of an older work.

Pamphlet (Booklet)

Education Committee. <u>Careers in Operations Research</u>.
    Baltimore: Operations Research Society of America,
    n.d.

A pamphlet is a small factual booklet, unbound, but usually stitched or stapled with or without a
paper cover and usually not more than about 50 pages. The notation "n.d." after the publisher's
name indicates that there was no date given for the publication date of the pamphlet. For another
example of a pamphlet, see the previous Hyman entry.

Foreword

Bellow, Saul. Foreword. <u>The Closing of the American
    Mind</u>. By Allan Bloom. New York: Simon, 1987.
    11-18.

A foreword, preface, and introduction are all examples of front matter in a book; an afterword, of
course, is back matter. They are all handled the same way in the works cited. A foreword (note
spelling) is a brief introductory piece, usually by someone other than the author; according to the
Chicago Manual of Style, the preface "normally runs only two to four pages" (19). Indicate the original author of the book after the title by preceding the author's full name with "By."

Preface

Lurie, Alison. Preface. <u>The Language of Clothes</u>. By
    Lurie. New York: Vintage-Random, 1981. ix-xi.

A preface is usually the author's informal introduction to the book. Since the preface is by Lurie, her last name preceded by the word "By" is all that is necessary.

Introduction

Sanders, Andrew. Introduction. <u>A Tale of Two Cities</u>.
    1859. By Charles Dickens. Oxford: Oxford UP, 1988.
    vii-xx.

An introduction can be a lengthy explanation of the direction of the book and is frequently the first portion of the text rather than a separate entity. It is written by the author or, if separate from the text as above, by an expert in the field.

Afterword

Fromm, Erich. Afterword. <u>1984</u>. 1949. By George Orwell.
    New York: Signet-NAL, 1961. 257-67.

An afterword is not very common (the word is not listed in one college dictionary and is treated briefly in two others), and the *Chicago Manual of Style* does not list it as a part of the normal back matter of a book; nevertheless, when it does appear, it is the author's or an expert commentator's concluding remarks about the book.

Reference Work

"Pantograph." <u>Webster's Third New International Diction-
    ary</u>, 1981 ed.

This is the unabridged dictionary of the G. & C. Merriam Company. Note that many dictionaries are called "Webster's" dictionaries [after Noah Webster (1758–1843)]; that is because the name is now in the public domain. Also, for a standard, non-specialized dictionary, give the term in quotation marks followed by the name of the book and the edition number and year of publication. No page number is necessary since words are alphabetized.

"Epistrophe." <u>Merriam-Webster's Collegiate Dictionary</u>.
    10th ed. 1994.

This is the Merriam Company's college dictionary.

"Hemisemidemiquaver." <u>American Heritage Dictionary</u>. 2nd
    College ed. 1982.

It is sometimes necessary to specify that the reference text is a "College" dictionary since publishing houses may publish several dictionaries with the same basic name.

"Redux." <u>Webster's New World Dictionary</u>. 3rd College
    ed. 1988.

"Anaphora." <u>Random House Webster's College Dictionary</u>.
    1991 ed.
Random House revised and retitled its college dictionary [formerly the *Random House College Dictionary*], and the new version is regarded as the first edition with this title.

"Psephology." <u>The Oxford Dictionary of English Etymol-
    ogy</u>. Ed. C.T. Onions. New York: Oxford UP, 1966.
This is an example of a specialized reference work; treat it as you would a regular book entry.

<u>Chicago Manual of Style</u>. 13th ed. Chicago: U of Chicago
    P, 1982.

<u>Publication Manual of the American Psychological Asso-
    ciation</u>. 4th ed. Washington, DC: American Psycho-
    logical Association, 1994.
Since there is no author listed for the above two reference works, begin with the title.

Carruth, Gorton. <u>Encyclopedia of American Facts and
    Dates</u>. 8th ed. New York: Harper, 1987.

Gibaldi, Joseph. <u>MLA Handbook for Writers of Research
    Papers</u>. 4th ed. New York: MLA, 1995.
If a publisher's acronym may be unfamiliar to your reader, spell it out but use abbreviations as necessary: Modern Lang. Assn.

Landis, Fred. "Vapor." <u>Funk & Wagnalls New
    Encyclopedia</u>. 1986 ed.
For unsigned encyclopedia articles, begin with the title of the entry. Signed articles, like the one above, contain the initials of the author in a contributor's section of the first volume; match the initials after the article with the initials in the contributor's section to find the full name and then supply that name as the first item in the works-cited entry.

"Birds." <u>Encyclopaedia Brittanica: Macropaedia</u>. 1990 ed.
"Birds" is a general category occupying the first 112 pages of volume 15 of the *Macropaedia;* if you want to refer to a specific article about bird behavior or habitat, list the author's name (coded by initials) along with the title of the specific article.

"Fair Labor Standards Act." <u>Microsoft Encarta '95</u>. CD-
    ROM, Redmond: Microsoft, 1994.

Annual Report

Cleveland State University. <u>Annual Report of Philan-
    thropy</u>. Cleveland: Cleveland State U, 1992.
Treat an annual report of a business or institution as you would a book.

Works-Cited Entries for Newspapers

Author Listed

Anderson, Kendall. "Archives Combed for Cherokee Ties."
    Dallas Morning News 3 July 1994: 49A, 52A.

Author Not Listed

"'Constructor' Program Shows Kids the Ropes." Sun Herald [North Olmsted, OH] 22 Apr. 1993: A7.

When the author is not listed, begin with the title and alphabetize in the works cited by the first important word of the title (not with a preposition ["about"] or an article ["the"]). Also, for a weekly paper that serves a number of communities, list only the home office after the paper's name.

Wire Service or Other Source, Author not Listed

Associated Press. "One Shuttle Comes Down, Another Prepares to Go Up." Plain Dealer [Cleveland] 18 Apr.
    1993: 18A.

A big-city newspaper might use a dozen or more sources for news; in the above Sunday paper, the *Plain Dealer* uses over 15 different sources in addition to its own staff. Examples of wire services are the Associated Press, Reuters, Newhouse News Service, and Scripps Howard. Examples of papers that provide news stories to other newspapers are the *New York Times, Washington Post,* and *Newsday*. Smaller newspapers, like the *Hartford Courant* and the *Register Herald of Beckley,* West Virginia, are also sources for news and feature stories. (Though the wire service listing is technically not required by the MLA system, the information that it provides is useful in assigning a source to cited material.)

Wire Service or Other Source, Author Listed

McAllister, Bill, Washington Post. "Commemorative Issue to Honor Dean Acheson." Plain Dealer [Cleveland]
    18 Apr. 1993: 9G.

Two or More Authors

Hunt, Albert R., and Carla Anne Robbins. "Gephardt Sees Russia Needing Prolonged Aid." Wall Street Journal
    13 Apr. 1993, midwest ed.: A3-4.

Carvahal, Doreen, Thuan Le, and Lily Dizon. "Southland Vietnamese Back Renewed Ties." Los Angeles Times
    12 June 1994: A1, A28.

Since news stories are usually not long, it is rare to see even two authors; nevertheless, when multiple authors occur, list them the same way you would for a book.

Columnist

Baker, Russell. "Prognosis: Unheavenly Dirt." <u>New York
    Times</u> 13 Apr. 1993, natl ed.: A13.

City, State, of Publication

Dixon, Jeff. "Land of Mottos and Egos." <u>Chicago Tribune</u>
    27 Oct. 1991, sec. 17: 1,5.

Leise, Cindy. "Historic Designation Sparks a Renova-
    tion." <u>Chronicle-Telegraph</u> [Elyria, OH] 12 Apr.
    1993: A1, A6.

When the place of publication is not part of the newspaper's name, enclose the city (and state's
two-letter postal abbreviation if necessary) within brackets after the name of the paper.

Edition

Fields, Gregg. "Companies Pitch to a Niche with Mar-
    lins." <u>Miami Herald</u> 18 Apr. 1993, Florida ed.: K1.

Specify the edition of the paper, if possible, since different editions will contain some different
material.

Editorial

"Growing Libraries." Editorial. <u>Morning Journal</u>
    [Lorain, OH] 18 Apr. 1993, Lorain County ed.: A4.

Letter to the Editor

Hutchinson, Kay Bailey. Letter. <u>Houston Chronicle</u> 26
    Feb. 1995: 3C.

Newspaper Article from a Database

Biddle, Frederic M. "TV Advertising Rates Showing Signs
    of a Slowdown." <u>Boston Globe</u> 7 Jan. 1990. <u>News-
    bank: Business and Economic Development</u> 21 (1990):
    fiche 10, grids E3-4.

Because Newsbank reformats original articles, the page numbers are not given; instead, give the
name of the database/vendor (Newsbank), the category (one of eighteen that Newsbank uses), the
volume number at the top of the fiche (convert the Roman numerals to Arabic), the year, the fiche
(microfilm sheet) number, and the location on the grid (one grid holds 98 pages: 7 vertical rows and
14 horizontal rows labeled with letters and numbers).

Book Review

Moore, Suzanne. "Clash of Symbols." Rev. of <u>Fads, Fash-
ions and Cults</u>, by Tony Thorne. <u>Sunday Times</u> [Lon-
don] 14 Apr. 1993, sec. 6: 10.

Play Review

Stearns, David Patrick. "'Horses': A Satisfying Day at
the Races." Rev. of <u>Three Men on a Horse</u>, by John
Cecil Holm and George Abbott. <u>USA Today</u> 14 Apr.
1993: 7D.

Music Review

Kozinn, Allan. "A Mendelssohn Oratorio." Rev. of
Mendelssohn's <u>St. Paul</u>. American Symphony Orches-
tra and Pro Arte Chorale. Carnegie Hall, New York.
<u>New York Times</u> 14 Apr. 1993, natl ed.: B2.

Dance Review

Salisbury, Wilma. "Choreographer Creates Fantasies."
Rev. of Feld Ballets/NY. Ohio Theater, Cleveland.
<u>Plain Dealer</u> [Cleveland] 19 Apr. 1993: 8E.

Works-Cited Entries for Magazines

Author Listed

Rybczynski, Witold. "The New Downtowns." <u>Atlantic
Monthly</u> May 1993: 98-106.

Author not Listed

"Which Cars Are Safest in a Crash." <u>Consumer Reports</u>
Apr. 1993: 199, 202.

Since there is no author listed, begin with the title of the article. Unlike most magazines, *Consumer Reports* paginates continuously through the volume year.

Two or More Authors

Hage, David, Sara Collins, and Warren Cohen with
        William J. Cook. "Austerity and Prosperity." <u>U.S.
        News and World Report</u> 29 Mar. 1993: 40-43.

Some newsmagazines list the primary author(s) and those who helped with reporting or research. An alternate form for four or more authors is to list only the first one followed by "et al.": Hage, David, et al.

Weekly Magazine

Angell, Roger. "Put Me in, Coach." <u>New Yorker</u> 3 May
        1993: 47-56,61-62.

All of pages 57–60 were taken up by a four-page advertisement. Sometimes, however, advertising pages in some magazines are not paginated and therefore are treated as if they were not there.

Zoglin, Richard. "Can Anybody Work This Thing?" <u>Time</u> 23
        Nov. 1992: 67.

Monthly Magazine

Wolkomir, Richard. "If Those Cobras Don't Get You, the
        Alligators Will." <u>Smithsonian</u> Nov. 1992: 166-76.

Vachon, Jane Mattern. "Should You Trust a Tail-Wagging
        Dog?" <u>Reader's Digest</u> Nov. 1992: 131-34.

Vass, George. "Is Major League Baseball on the Brink of
        Revolution?" <u>Baseball Digest</u> Feb. 1993: 31-40.

"The 3 Biggest Exercise Mistakes." <u>McCall's</u> Nov. 1994:
        40. <u>Infotrac: Health Reference Center</u>. CD-ROM.
        Information Access. Feb. 1995.

After the regular magazine entry, add the name of the database (Infotrac), the title of the section from which the information is derived (Health Reference Center), the delivery medium (CD-ROM), the name of the vendor (Information Access), and the date of the database (Feb. 1995).

Letter to the Editor

Schlack, Lawrence B. Letter. <u>World Monitor</u> Nov. 1992: 5.

Terms like Letter, Editorial, Table, Map, Cartoon, etc. are neither underlined nor set off by quotation marks because they are descriptive terms and not titles.

Movie Review

Gleiberman, Owen. "Crazy for You." Rev. of <u>Benny and
    Joon</u>, dir. Jeremiah Chechick. <u>Entertainment Weekly</u>
    23 Apr. 1993: 36-37.

Kael, Pauline. Rev. of <u>The Grapes of Wrath</u>, dir. John
    Ford. <u>Microsoft Cinemania '94</u>. CD-ROM. Redmond:
    Microsoft, 1993.

Book Review

Jenkyns, Richard. "Hat Trick." Rev. of <u>The Man in the
    Bowler Hat</u>, by Fred Miller Robinson. <u>New Yorker</u> 10
    May 1993: 109-12.

Klinkenborg, Verlyn. Rev. of <u>Anthony Trollope</u>, by Vic-
    toria Glendinning. <u>Smithsonian</u> Apr. 1993: 156-59.
Since *Smithsonian*'s book reviews do not have individual titles, begin with "Rev. of"

Music Review of a Record, Tape, or Compact Disc

Nash, Alanna. "Lovely, Patty." Rev. of <u>Only What I
    Feel</u>, by Patty Loveless. <u>Entertainment Weekly</u> 23
    Apr. 1993: 36-37.

Interview, Question-and-Answer Format

Lee, Spike. Interview. <u>Time</u> 23 Nov. 1992: 66.
For a Personal Interview and Telephone Interview, see the Other Sources section that follows.

Specially Titled Department of a Magazine

"Talk of the Town." <u>New Yorker</u> 3 May 1993: 33-37.
Other examples would be "*Harper*'s Index" and the *Atlantic*'s "745 Boylston Street."

Works-Cited Entries for Scholarly or Professional Journals

Single Author, Each Issue Continuously Paginated

Tobin, Gary Allan. "The Bicycle Boom of the 1890's: The
    Development of Private Transportation and the
    Birth of the Modern Tourist." <u>Journal of Popular
    Culture</u> 7.4 (1974): 838-49.
This example also illustrates the use of a subtitle, an issue number following the volume number, the
year of publication, and, since the page numbers are so high, the fact that this journal is continuously

paginated. Technically, all that is needed is the volume number, year of publication, and page numbers to locate the article in a continuously paginated journal, but extra information (issue number, month or season of publication) just makes it easier to locate the article.

```
Williams, Nancy. "Research as a Process: A Transac-
     tional Approach." Journal of Teaching Writing 7.2
     (Fall/Winter 1988): 193-204.
```
Note that three digits are used when going from one hundred to two hundred.

```
Melchior, Bonnie. "Teaching Paradise Lost: The Unfortu-
     nate Fall." College Literature 14.1 (Winter 1987):
     76-84.
```
Underline the title of a long poem, like *Paradise Lost* above.

```
Iyasere, Marla Mudar. "Beyond the Mechanical: Technical
     Writing Revisited." Journal of Advanced Composi-
     tion 5 (1984): 173-80.
```

Single Author, Each Issue Paged Anew

```
Colby, Joan. "Math Anxiety." Memphis State Review. 3.2
     (Spring 1983): 14.
```
When each issue is paged anew, you must include at least the volume number and issue number (you may also include the season or month for ease in locating the issue although it isn't necessary).

An Article from an Online Database

```
Brent, Douglas A. "Information Technology and the
     Breakdown of 'Places' of Knowledge." EJournal 4.4
     (1994): n. pag. Online Internet. 21 Mar. 1995.
```
After the regular journal entry, add pagination information ("n. pag." means that the article was not paginated), the delivery medium (Online), the computer network (Internet), and the date of access (21 Mar. 1995).

An Article from a Portable Database

```
Marwick, Charles. "New Telecommunications Relay Ser-
     vices, Other Communication Advances, Will Aid Dis-
     abled People." JAMA 270 (1993): 1168-69. Infotrac:
     Health Reference Center. CD-ROM. Information
     Access. Feb. 1995.
```
After the regular journal entry, add the name of the database (Infotrac), the title of the section from which the information is derived (Health Reference Center), the delivery medium (CD-ROM), the name of the vendor (Information Access), and the date of the database (Feb. 1995).

Two or More Authors

Boston, Louise, and Edward J. McNeeley. "Computer
    Memory." <u>Gamut</u> 13 (Fall 1984): 76-79.

The above journal does not use volume numbers, only issue numbers; therefore, treat each issue as a separate volume paged anew with each issue.

Book Review

Dimock, Wai-chee. Rev. of <u>Subversive Genealogy: The
    Politics and Art of Herman Melville</u>, by Michael
    Paul Rogin. <u>Georgia Review</u> 37.4 (Winter 1983):
    912-14.

Interview, Question-and-Answer Format

Pinsker, Sanford. "Speaking about Short Fiction: An
    Interview with Joyce Carol Oates." <u>Studies in
    Short Fiction</u> 18.3 (Summer 1981): 239-43.

The word *Interview* is normally placed before the title, but since in the above example *Interview* is contained within the subtitle, it would be a needless repetition to place it in its normal position.

Other Sources

Advertisement (Print)

"One Gallon per Second." Goodyear Aquatred. Advertise-
    ment. <u>U.S. News and World Report</u> 21 June 1993: 21.

Advertisement (Television)

"Phone First." Ohio Bell. Advertisement. WKYC-TV,
    Cleveland. 11:34 p.m., 22 June 1993.

For advertisements, try to identify them by a title (if they have one) or a theme.

Almanac

"Energy." <u>The World Almanac and Book of Facts 1993</u>. Ed.
    Mark S. Hoffman. New York: Pharos, 1992: 169-75.

Providing the section in quotation marks and inclusive page numbers at the end makes it easy to locate the information. Note that this entry is like a chapter in a book.

Artwork (Viewed in Person)

```
da Vinci, Leonardo. Mona Lisa. Musée du Louvre, Paris.
```
Add the date of the visit if it is important to your study.

Artwork (Viewed in a Book)

```
da Vinci, Leonardo. Mona Lisa. Musée du Louvre, Paris.
     Plate 644 in History of Art. 4th ed. By H. W. Janson
     and Anthony F. Janson. New York: Abrams; Englewood
     Cliffs, NJ: Prentice, 1991.
```
When two publishing houses produce a book, both are listed and separated by a semicolon.

Bible

```
The Bible. Jerusalem Version.
```
Do not underline sacred texts; indicate the version of the Bible (King James, New American, etc.).
The in-text citation will contain chapter and verse: (Gen. 9:1–5), (Matt. 18:21–22).

Class Lecture

```
Smythe, John. Class Lecture. City College. Kingston,
     PA. 27 Nov. 1992.
```

Computer Service

```
"Study Links Stress, Heart Attacks." Prodigy Interac-
     tive Personal Service. Online. Prodigy. 21 Mar.
     1995.
```
For a commercial computer service such as Prodigy, America Online, CompuServe, etc. give the author, if available, the title of the information, the date of the information if different from the access date, the delivery medium (Online), the name of the database (Prodigy Interactive Personal Service), the vendor (Prodigy), and the date of access (21 Mar. 1995).

Computer Software

```
Word for Windows. Vers. 6.0. Computer software.
     Microsoft, 1993-94. MS-DOS 3.1, Windows 3.1.
```
Provide basic requirements for the software to run.

Computer Software Manual

```
Microsoft Word User's Guide. Vers. 6.0. Redmond:
     Microsoft, 1993-94.
```

Concert (in Person)

Pavarotti, Luciano. Concert. Central Park, New York. 26
June 1993.

Concert (on Television)

Pavarotti, Luciano. Concert. Central Park, New York.
PBS. WVIZ-TV, Cleveland. 26 June 1993.

Government Documents / Legal Citations

16 US Code. Sec. 4601-6a(b). 1965.
The citation above refers to a section of Title 16 of the United States Code that deals with the Land
and Water Conservation Act of 1965.

Ohio Revised Code. Sec. 3313.60.
This section of the Ohio Revised Code prescribes the course of graded study for Ohio schools.

Cong. Rec. 23 June 1993: S7756-64.
Preceding the page numbers is the letter S for the Senate [H for the House]. The *Congressional
Record* is published daily and has continuous pagination.

Marbury v. Madison. 1803.
Judicial review is established by this famous Supreme Court decision.

Interview (Television or Radio)

Pavarotti, Luciano. Interview. Charlie Rose. PBS. WVIZ-
TV, Cleveland. 22 June 1993.

Interview (Print)

Lee, Spike. Time. 23 Nov. 1992: 66.

Interview (in Person or via Telephone)

Smythe, Mary. Manager, Ajax Mfg. Chicago. Personal
Interview. 18 Dec. 1991.
If the person interviewed is not well-known or pertinent background information is not given fully in
the text, then provide it in the works-cited citation, although, strictly speaking, all that is necessary is
the person's name, type of interview (personal interview or telephone interview), and date.

Letter to Author

Smythe, John. Letter to Author. 21 Jan. 1990.

Motion Picture

<u>Indiana Jones and the Last Crusade</u>. Dir. Stephen
    Spielberg. Perf. Harrison Ford, Sean Connery,
    Denholm Elliott, Alison Doody, John Rhys-Davies,
    and Julian Glover. Paramount, 1989. 126 min.

Play

<u>The Mousetrap</u>. By Agatha Christie. Huntington Play-
    house, Bay Village, OH. 20 Sep. 1992. Based on
    Agatha Christie's story "Three Blind Mice."
If needed, additional information goes after the date, as above.

<u>Damn Yankees</u>. By George Abbott and Douglas Wallop.
    Perf. Gwen Verdon, Stephen Douglass, and Ray Wal-
    ston. Forty-Sixth Street Theatre, New York. 5 May
    1955.

Recording

Kanawa, Kiri Te. <u>Kiri Sings Gershwin</u>. New Princess
    Theater Orchestra. Cond. John McGlinn. EMI
    Digital, 1987.
If the recording is on a medium other than compact disc (CD), specify the medium (audiocassette, audiotape, or LP) after the title.

Seger, Bob. "Old Time Rock and Roll." <u>Stranger in Town</u>.
    Audiocassette. Bob Seger and the Silver Bullet
    Band. Capitol, 1978.

Television Program

"World Trade Center: Ground Zero." <u>Nightline</u>. With Ted
    Koppel. ABC. WEWS-TV, Cleveland. 16 June 1993.
If a program has an episode title or program title, place it before the name of the program itself.

Richard Lewis. <u>Late Night with David Letterman</u>. NBC.
    WKYC-TV, Cleveland. 16 June 1993.
Use this form to cite a guest on a program.

Tables, Surveys, Figures, Questionnaires, Interviews

Tables and figures are ways of providing visual information to your reader. A **table** is an arrangement of numerical information in columns. It is preceded by the table number and the title (the description of what the table contains). If you as the source produce the data and configure the table, then nothing appears below the table. If, however, you used data prepared from another source, then you list that source following the tabular material in footnote form, like this:

Source: Mari Smythe, A Collector's Price Guide to Victorian Art (New York: Ulysses Press, 1888) 25.

In a **survey**, you gather data by observation or inquiry in order to get an answer to a question. Let's say that you want to find out whether people really do obey a law or to what degree they do. Drivers are supposed to stop when they see a stop sign. But do they actually stop? To find out, we analyzed the traffic behavior of 200 drivers as they approached a three-way stop in a residential area of Northeastern Ohio where the speed limit was 25 miles per hour.

Each driver was evaluated on a one-to-five scale. A "1" would be given to a driver who totally ignored the stop sign (i.e., did not even slow down), but we did not see any of these; a "2" was given to drivers who slowed minimally and who surely would have been cited if a police officer were present; a "3" was given to drivers who slowed significantly but did not come close to stopping; a "4-" was given to drivers who clearly deserved more than a "3" but who did not come close enough to a stop to be awarded a "4+", which was given to drivers who very nearly came to a stop (this we called a "virtual stop"); a "5" was given to drivers who obeyed the letter of the law by coming to a complete stop.

The table shown below summarizes the results. For each direction is listed the number and **percentage** of drivers earning each rating as well as the average rating.

Table 6.1

Traffic Survey of 200 Cars Approaching a Three-Way Stop

Direction, 1–5 Rating, **Percent**, Average Rating

		1		2		3		4-		4+		5	Avg
W to East	0	**0%**	2	**2.6%**	26	**33.8%**	41	**53.2%**	7	**9.1%**	1	**1.3%**	3.48
S to North	0	**0%**	9	**8.3%**	42	**38.9%**	38	**35.2%**	16	**14.8%**	3	**2.8%**	3.40
N to South	0	**0%**	1	**6.7%**	4	**26.7%**	7	**46.7%**	2	**13.3%**	1	**6.7%**	3.56
Total	0	**0%**	12	**6.0%**	72	**36.0%**	86	**43.0%**	25	**12.5%**	5	**2.5%**	3.44

The information presented in Table 6.1 is useful because it surveys a sufficient number of cars for a pattern to emerge. As a rule of thumb, one hundred samples should be the minimum so that your margin of error would not be too great. When polling organizations produce the results of their surveys, you will usually see numbers ranging from about 600 to 1500. The greater the number, the greater the accuracy. But, obviously, you can't survey those numbers for a research paper.

A **figure** is graphic material used to illustrate something in your text. It can be a drawing, diagram, chart, graph, photograph, or cartoon. It differs from a table in that the caption appears below the illustration and to the right of the figure designation. Again, if you are the source of both the illustration and the information, you do not list yourself as the source (Remember that *what is not attributed to someone else is attributed to you*). If, on the other hand, you are using data and/or illustrations from another source, then list the source as in the example in Table 6.1, in footnote form. What follows is an example of a figure where the author configured the illustrative material from the data provided by another source:

> Economic history was made during the 1930's but in a negative way. If we take a look at the unemployment statistics for the United States during that decade, we can see why the period is referred to as the Great Depression, a decade-long period of economic crisis and the search for economic prosperity. Figure 6.1 shows that unemployment ranged from 8.7 percent in 1930 to a high of 24.9 percent in 1933:

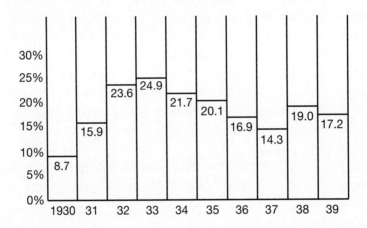

Figure 6.1 Unemployment Statistics. Source: <u>World Almanac and Book of Facts</u> 1994. Ed. Robert Famighetti (Mahwah, NJ: Funk & Wagnalls, 1993) 130.

A **questionnaire** is a written document that elicits answers to carefully constructed questions that can be tabulated easily and accurately. Many times questionnaires will have five or six choices ranging from, for example, "strongly agree" to "strongly disagree," with intermediate steps, almost like an academic grading system that ranges from A to F. If you ask open-ended questions, on the other hand, you will have difficulty categorizing the answers even though the responses might be useful. (Open-ended questions produce results more like those from an interview than from a questionnaire or survey.) Here are examples of two different kinds of questionnaires with a few sample questions included:

1. There is too much violence on television.

Strongly agree	Agree	Neutral	Disagree	Strongly disagree
1	2	3	4	5

2. Violence on television causes anti-social behavior.

Strongly agree	Agree	Neutral	Disagree	Strongly disagree
1	2	3	4	5

3. Steps should be taken to reduce television violence.

Strongly agree	Agree	Neutral	Disagree	Strongly disagree
1	2	3	4	5

Or, each question might have a different set of answers:

1. When you have the opportunity to select a name-brand product in a store or a generic product of the same type and size, which do you buy?

    (a) Name brand   (b) Generic

2. Do you feel that generic soft drinks taste as good as name-brand soft drinks?

    (a) Yes   (b) No

Although **interviews** are time consuming to conduct, they can be useful tools in gathering information for a research paper. The personal, face-to-face interview, the interview conducted over the telephone, and the printed interview in question-and-answer format comprise the three basic types that are frequently used in research papers as primary sources. When you are conducting an interview, prepare for it beforehand by writing down good questions: *why* questions elicit reasons, causation; *what* questions, factual information; *how* questions, process; *who,* agency; *when,* temporality, and *where,* location. Remember that unsubstantiated opinion is useless and that even expert opinion may be dismissed as "that's only one person's opinion on the subject"; so, as a general rule, it is better to gather facts rather than opinion.

In short, surveys and questionnaires, if done scientifically, can give you accurate data; interviews, since they elicit individual responses, will not be scientific but can be useful for their facts and interesting for their opinions.

Exercise 6.2: This exercise deals with elements of the research paper that are crucial to its success: paraphrasing and documentation.

1. In the following excerpt from Thomas Henry Huxley's writings, the British biologist and popularizer of Darwin explains the scientific method and the necessity for rigorous inquiry. Write a regular paraphrase of Huxley's ideas.

   In scientific inquiry it becomes a matter of duty to expose a supposed law to every possible verification, and to take care, moreover, that this is done intentionally, and not left to mere accident.... And in science, as in common life, our confidence in a law is in exact proportion to the absence of variation in the result of our experimental verifications. For instance, if you let go your grasp of an article you may have in your hand, it will immediately fall to the ground. That is a very common verification of one of the best established laws of nature—that of gravitation.

2. The following is an excerpt from an essay on superstition that appeared in *The Spectator* in 1711. Write a summary paraphrase of Joseph Addison's commentary:

   Upon my Return Home, I fell into a profound Contemplation on the Evils that Attend these superstitious Follies of Mankind; how they subject us to imaginary Afflictions, and additional Sorrows, that do not properly come within our Lot. As if the natural Calamities of Life were not sufficient for it, we turn the most indifferent Circumstances into Misfortunes, and suffer as much from trifling Accidents, as from real Evils. I have known the shooting of a Star spoil a Night's Rest; and have seen a Man in Love grow pale and lose his Appetite, upon the plucking of a Merry-thought. A Screech-Owl at Midnight has alarm'd a family, more than a Band of Robbers; nay, the Voice of a Cricket hath struck more Terror than the Roaring of a Lion. There is nothing so inconsiderable, which may not appear dreadful to an imagination that is filled with Omens and Prognosticks. A rusty Nail, or a crooked Pin, shoot up into Prodigies.

3. Write a works-cited entry from the following information (Hint: one piece of information is not needed).

   Author: Bill James Blackburn
   Article title: Waving the Flag
   Article subtitle: An Assessment of Patriotic Fervor
   Journal: American Political Science
   Volume: Six
   Issue number: Five
   Pages: 29, 30, 31, 32, 33
   Journal editor: Samuel Wordsmith
   Year of publication: 1991

Chapter 7

Putting It All Together: Rough Draft to Final Product

Writing is more than applying a mechanical device to form symbols on a medium. A computer, typewriter, or pen can do that. Real writing is produced by the intelligence behind the device: a human person who has something to say. Since writing is a social act, we write because we want to do something for somebody, such as explain, inform, clarify, exhort, amuse, inspire, or convince. And writing a research paper is an important way to do that since it is the sharing of a discovery. If we are sharing the results of our study with the reader, we should, as we shall see, be attentive to the needs of our audience. Making a discovery means that we have uncovered information worth looking at, something new that has not appeared in quite the same form that we now see it because of the application of our own intelligence in synthesizing the research materials. There is, perhaps, even an element of surprise and pleasure that goes along with our discovery. Thus both elements—discovering and sharing—are essential ingredients to the success of the research paper.

If the successful research paper is our goal, then we want to map our route toward it to avoid the bottlenecks that slow us down (such as putting off today what we can do tomorrow); we want to be wary of shortcuts that become dead ends (not thoroughly evaluating secondary and even primary sources but using them anyway because time is running out); and we want to keep track of our time so that we can do our best work without being harassed by the clock because time *is* running out. In brief, writing a research paper should be an enjoyable, though challenging, adventure, not an unavoidable ordeal. Let's review the steps that can get us off to a good start.

Working with Your Topic

First, read through the entire topic list and then select one that you are interested in or would like to learn more about. Each of the fifty topics allows for your unique and specific approach; therefore, come up with an angle that will present your findings effectively. Throughout this aspect of topic refinement and individualization, you will be asking questions and getting answers, posing hypotheses and testing them so that your paper will be thoughtful, authoritative, and helpful to the reader.

Determining the Audience

Since you are writing for others, you will want to give some consideration to the question of audience, or readership. You naturally would adjust your writing style to accommodate those who would be most receptive to what you had to say. If your readers were boy scouts, for example, your diction, tone, and style would be different from the approach you would use if your audience were chemists or cultural anthropologists. Look at it in a different way: if you wished to send your paper to a journal for publication, you would want to look at a copy of the periodical to see what style it had been written in and to whom it appealed. Jack London provides us with a good example of how an author can use different voices to suit his audience. Two versions of London's famous short story "To Build a Fire" have been published. The first version appeared in 1902 in a boys' magazine called *Youth's Companion,* and it is a good deal shorter and simpler and more didactic than the more famous version that was based on it and published six years later in a general circulation magazine. Though you may not be sending your paper off to be published, the London example is instructive: writers tailor their material to their readers' backgrounds and interests to communicate most effectively. Therefore, it would be a good idea to look at some professional journals to see the style that researchers use in the discipline you've chosen to write your paper.

Ordering Your Ideas

The next step in the preparation stage is making an outline of your ideas. As we mentioned in Chapter Four, the outline can take many different shapes: at the beginning it might be a rough sketch of main ideas that develops into a formal outline that logically divides sometimes unrelated units of research material into smaller, more manageable, and more cohesive subunits of facts and opinions. As your paper takes shape, the outline will become a useful tool that will direct both you and your reader through your paper and will serve, ultimately, as a table of contents.

Perhaps the last thing you will do, if you haven't done it already, is to formulate a plan of attack: Why are you writing this paper? What major insight will you provide your reader? What statement can tie together all the information and speculations that you have made thus far? Your answer is called a thesis statement or controlling idea. It usually appears in the first part of your paper, usually at the end of your introduction. Your introduction can be one paragraph or several paragraphs depending on the overall length of the research paper. You will then develop it in the body of the paper with primary and secondary support, and reaffirm your main ideas at the end of your paper.

Remember that your thesis statement should really say something. It should not be too general (Movies are better than ever) or too obvious (Television has both positive and negative effects). Do not substitute a rhetorical method for the thesis (I will compare city life to country life), because this simply announces a process and is therefore not a thesis. Rather, be specific and concrete since that creates interest (The shot clock works to the advantage of the stronger collegiate basketball team). Or, try offering a solution to a problem (Removing "D" and "F" grades and substituting "No Credit" for them will change the traditional "A-B-C-D-F" letter-grade system into a positive assessment tool for the colleges). Finally, be prepared to defend the thesis statement in your paper with facts, statistics, opinions, and solid reasoning on your part.

Writing and Revising

After you have collected all your data and written your notes, you will use your outline to guide you in writing the first draft of your paper. It's a good idea to write the first draft all the way through so you can get your ideas down completely and in the order you want to present them. Don't worry too much about style at this point; that can come later. Let's say you were writing your paper about the continuing popularity of denim jeans. You might start your paper with some interesting statistics about jeans (how many were sold last year, for example) to show how all-pervasive they are in our culture. This will lead you into identifying your purpose in writing—that denim jeans are more than a garment but a political, social, and cultural statement firmly rooted in the American tradition. You will then go on to develop your ideas concretely in the paragraphs that follow.

Revising the Introduction

An introduction should engage the reader's interest. Memory expert Tony Buzan [*Make the Most of Your Mind*. New York: Linden Press-Simon, 1984, 40.] reminds us that first, last, and unusual things create an impression on us and stick with us. But how do you engage the reader's interest? You can cite statistics—people love to hear numbers and their significance (batting averages, Gallup polls, Nielsen ratings, the price of gold, etc.). People are also interested in stories, so you might begin with an anecdote. Or you can quote from an authority because people are interested in others' opinions. These lead-ins must not be gratuitous—that is, they must be relevant to your purpose, and they must lead to your purpose. Next, you may want to give a little background on your topic and then finally give a directional signal as to where you will be taking your reader in your paper. The directional signal can be straight forward and complete, in which case you will tell the reader essentially what your conclusion is and what your findings are. This is a deductive method, where your ideas develop from a general statement—actually the thesis—supported by particular examples. Or, your directional signal may show the direction without giving the destination. This is an inductive method, where your particular supportive evidence leads inevitably to your conclusion—actually the fully delineated thesis statement. This latter approach creates interest through the suspense of an unfurling resolution.

Revising the Body of the Paper

The body of the research paper is the heart of your presentation and should consist of sufficiently developed paragraphs that support each of the points of your outline. In many cases, the topic sentence for each paragraph is placed as the first sentence, because the first position, as we have seen, is the most important and most memorable, and everything that follows it should support it with details that are concrete and specific and reasoning that is well thought out and compelling. Make sure that you go over each body paragraph to remove vague statements and replace them with clear, concise, and concrete statements; insert bridge words, such as *moreover, next, in like manner,* or *to be sure,* that connect ideas for clarity; remove sentences that do not support your main idea or that get off the track; and add new material where necessary to strengthen your paper.

Introduce your sources and integrate them into the discussion. Making introductions smooth and seamless is one of the most difficult stylistic operations a researcher will perform. Furthermore, the readability of your paper depends not only on the materials that you assemble, present, and evaluate, but also on how you do this. Certainly, your paper must be informative, but it must be interesting as well. Here is an example that creates interest as it develops.

> In 1948, because of a scarcity of natural resources, Illinois produced license plates made of soybeans. *Chicago Tribune* writer Jeff Dixon noted that the soybean plates "were fine except for one thing—cows kept eating them"(5).

As you collect facts and opinions, don't lean too heavily on secondary and tertiary sources. Don't overlook the primary sources all around you. For example, if you were advocating better eating habits for school children, the newly devised "food pyramid" could be used as a source as well as the "nutrition facts" labels now required on packaged foods. Also, if you think ads for too many non-nutritious foods are being aimed at children, turn on your VCR, tape them, count them, time them, evaluate them, and then use the data in your paper. Another suggestion while you are doing the research paper is to read the daily papers from your city, *USA Today,* the *New York Times,* and the *Wall Street Journal*. Assuredly, there will be some information that you will be able to use in the six weeks or so that you will be collecting information for your paper. If you look at some or all of these periodicals, if not daily, then with sufficient frequency to generate usable information, you will be processing more data that will in turn help you to produce a more thoughtful paper. The more you read, the more you will know, and the more you will want to share that knowledge.

Revising the Conclusion

The conclusion of the research paper should not be contained solely in the last paragraph. You should be coming to conclusions throughout the paper, especially in the last half of the paper. It is true that a concluding paragraph will wrap up your paper and give it a sense of completeness, but this is only the last paragraph of the conclusion itself, which may consist of several paragraphs.

The revising stage is not complete until you're pretty well satisfied with what you've done. Thus you might end up with several drafts of your paper because you went over it several times, each time trying to make it clearer, sharper, and, in a word, better.

The Final Product: A Sample Paper in MLA Style

The sample research paper that follows conforms to Modern Language Association (MLA) style in its documentation format. The marginal notations will give you some tips that should make the writing of your paper a little less daunting.

Sample Paper in MLA Style

Steinbeck's <u>The Grapes of Wrath</u>

as a Mirror of the Great Depression

Student's Name

Professor's Name

Course Number

Date Turned In

Center the title about two inches from the top; place your name in the center of the page; and center the professor's name, course number, and date about two inches from the bottom of the paper.

Outline

Thesis: John Steinbeck's <u>The Grapes of Wrath</u> was an accurate account of the times and the social conse- quences of the Great Depression and is historically significant for us today.

Double space the outline throughout.

Introduction: Steinbeck's <u>The Grapes of Wrath</u> (novel and movie) as a mirror of the Great Depression

   I. Criteria for determining Steinbeck's accuracy

      A. Not only a writer but an observer

      B. Educated by the events of the time

      C. Historical accuracy

  II. Reception of the book

      A. Steinbeck's concerns and precautions

For a sentence outline, see pages 35–36.

      B. Associated Farmers' campaign in California

      C. McWilliams' defense of Steinbeck's depiction

      D. Franklin and Eleanor Roosevelt's reactions

      E. Three phases of literary criticism

          1. 1940-55: Accuracy and credentials

          2. 1955-73: Literary values

          3. 1973-89: Biographical and regional fields

Student's Name   ii

III.   Comparison of novel to the works of three

historians

A.   John Kenneth Galbraith--economic portrayal

B.   Frederick Lewis Allen--social perspective

1.   Description of the Dust Bowl

2.   Social-historical analysis

C.   Richard Hofstadter--political view

IV.   Need for social reform in 1930's and today

A.   Robert Brustein on the Broadway play

B.   Oral historian Studs Terkel's comments

Conclusion: Steinbeck's novel reflects the economic,

social, and political plight of the Okies during the

Depression and provides the reader with insights into

the continual need for reform to create a better life

for the "underprivileged" in the 1930's as well as

today.

Student's Name   1

Steinbeck's <u>The Grapes of Wrath</u>

as a Mirror of the Great Depression

Published in 1939, John Steinbeck's <u>The Grapes of Wrath</u> was considered the "biggest literary event of the year" (Wyatt 2), hitting the top of the best-seller list in May. The movie came out in 1940. John Ford won an academy award for best director and Jane Darwell, who played Mama, won one for best supporting actress. The novel, which also won the National Book Award and the Pulitzer Prize that year, tells the story of a migrant family and the difficulties they experience on their way to and in California. More importantly, Steinbeck's <u>The Grapes of Wrath</u> was an accurate historical account of the consequences of the Great Depression and remains historically significant for us today.

Steinbeck's accuracy in reporting these conditions has been debated for half a century (Wyatt 13). Determining Steinbeck's accuracy involves examining his credentials and experience as a writer and observer, the reception and other analyses of the

Use one-inch margins on all four sides and place your last name and page number on each page one-half inch from the top.

Common knowledge information need not be documented.

Thesis is stated here, following the introductory material.

MS Style: Place only one space after all marks of punctuation.

Student's Name   2

book, and how the book compares with historians'
accounts.

Prior to writing <u>The Grapes of Wrath</u>, Steinbeck
had published several novels, including <u>Cup of Gold</u>
and <u>The Pastures of Heaven</u>. "Steinbeck first dealt
with . . . social themes associated with most of his
works" ("Steinbeck" 343). In addition to being a
writer, Steinbeck was also an observer; he had been
born in and had lived in Salinas, California (Owens
xi). Having lived in California and already having
written several works gave Steinbeck an excellent
background for writing this epic.

Steinbeck was also "educated" by the events of
the time. He agreed in 1936 "to do a series of articles [on the migrant workers called 'The Harvest Gyp-
sies'] for the <u>San Francisco News</u>" (Owens 3). Addi-
tionally, he traveled around with Tom Collins, who
was the first camp manager in California. Collins'
reports "provided the novelist with a fund of migrant
behavior and lore" (Wyatt 13). Steinbeck's beliefs
were affected by his experiences in learning about

*This second
paragraph serves
as an amplification
of the thesis.*

*Use brackets for
your own
commentary
within the direct
quotation.*

the migrant workers. The novel, comments Kurt
Hochenauer, can also be read as the education of Tom
Joad, "who sets up one of the novel's major themes--
the poor versus the rich . . ." (393-94).

So Steinbeck learned first-hand about the social
ills of the Depression, including disillusionment.
This is reflected in his writing. For example, in <u>Of
Mice and Men</u>, the reader watches the dreams of George
and Lennie evaporate; in "The Chrysanthemums," Elisa
Allen has her image of proud strength shattered; and
in <u>The Grapes of the Wrath</u>, the Joads are deprived of
their glorious image of California as they realize it
is not the land of opportunity but rather the land of
exploitation. In <u>The Grapes of Wrath</u>, Steinbeck con-
veyed the desperation felt by the migrant workers.
But he strove to be accurate.

Steinbeck himself said, "I'm trying to write
history while it is happening and I don't want to be
wrong" (<u>Letters</u> 162). He acknowledged to Elizabeth
Otis, his literary representative, that this would
"not be a popular book" because of its contents, but

The ellipses (three spaced periods) indicate that something has been left out of the direct quotation. A fourth period (or other terminal mark of punctuation) ends the sentence and is placed after the parenthetical notation.

This quotation is an example of the use of primary material: Steinbeck's Letters.

Student's Name   4

Steinbeck refused to make adjustments in his book to
placate the publisher and readers (<u>Letters</u> 173, 175).

Despite his intense desire to portray the influx
of migrant workers accurately, Steinbeck was concerned about how his book would be received. Though
he did not change the book around, he took precau-
tions to make sure that "things [were] thoroughly
documented and the materials turned over to . . . the
Attorney General" and certain information was given
to J. Edgar Hoover in case "I take a nose dive" (<u>Let-
ters</u> 187). Steinbeck also feared a smear attempt; he
was warned by an undersheriff of Santa Clara County
not to "go into any hotel room alone" because a "dame
[would] come in, tear off her clothes, scratch her
face and scream" (<u>Letters</u> 187).

While people did not agree on whether or not <u>The
Grapes of Wrath</u> was accurate or appropriate, nobody
could refute that it created a controversy. David
Wyatt reports, "Feeling ran highest in Oklahoma and
California" (2). In California, he notes, the Associ-
ated Farmers organized a campaign that refuted

These are examples of primary sources being used.

Steinbeck's charges by telling people that everything was great and that the "Grapes of Gladness" was a more fitting description for the condition of the workers (2).

However, writer and farm-labor expert Carey McWilliams defended Steinbeck's novel:

> By 1942, in an essay entitled "California Pastoral," Carey McWilliams laid to rest all charges of inaccuracy in The Grapes of Wrath, marshalling overwhelming evidence of the novel's honesty in depicting the conditions in California's fields during the thirties. (Owens 5)

Direct quotations of five or more lines are set off by indenting ten spaces (one inch) from the left-hand margin. The right-hand margin stays the same as the rest of the paper.

This controversy even reached the White House. After reading The Grapes of Wrath, President Franklin Roosevelt said over the radio that "500,000 Americans . . . live in the covers of that book" (qtd. in Wyatt 3). Moreover, First Lady Eleanor Roosevelt, after touring the migrant camps in California, said, "I never have thought The Grapes of Wrath was exaggerated" (qtd. in Letters 202).

This paragraph contains examples of tertiary sources. Use "qtd. in" before the sources in which they were located.

Student's Name   6

In addition to political analysis, there was also a literary debate. Wyatt identifies three phases for literary criticism from 1940-89. The first (1940-55) involved analyzing the work for accuracy and also scrutinizing the credentials of the author. The second (1955-73) focused on the novel's literary values as opposed to political concerns. And in the third (1973-89) the book was "framed by its biographical and regional fields of force" (4).

In the 1990's the basis of determining the book's validity lies in its historical accuracy, how Steinbeck's analysis compares with what historians have had to say concerning the Great Depression, the Dust Bowl, the migrant workers, and life in California.[1] Steinbeck inserted general chapters into The Grapes of Wrath; these serve as a commentary, not directly related to the plot itself, on the impact of the time's events. These intercalary chapters serve as a basis for comparison with historians' accounts.

Writing in The Great Crash, John Kenneth Galbraith cites five reasons for the onset of the

This paragraph utilizes secondary source materials.

Student's Name   7

The use of material by Galbraith, Allen, and Hofstadter, though not related directly to Steinbeck's novel, provides historical background for the research paper.

Depression. These were bad distribution of income, bad corporate structure, bad banking structure, foreign imbalance, and lack of economic intelligence (182). After the Depression, the farmers lost their land to banks, insurance companies, and investors. Steinbeck describes the Depression's dire consequences for the farmers; he shows the results of these economic conditions. In chapter five of <u>The Grapes of Wrath</u>, Steinbeck refers to the bank as a "monster" unlike a man. "The bank, the fifty-thousand-acre owner, can't be responsible. You're on land that isn't yours" (43-44). Steinbeck discusses the bad banking structure, saying that the banks were concerned only for profits and not about the well-being of the former owners.

In <u>Since Yesterday</u>, Frederick Lewis Allen describes America in the thirties. Interestingly, Allen's account of the Dust Bowl is very similar to Steinbeck's. Allen observes, "In 1934 and 1935 Californians became aware of an increasing influx into their state of families and groups of families of

Student's Name   8

'Okies" (160). Allen's historical analysis corre-
sponds with what Steinbeck says, but Steinbeck ani-
mates and personalizes his account, extending it over
several chapters. For example, in chapter seven,
Steinbeck describes a likely scenario in the sale of
a car: "Goin' to California? Here's jus' what you
need. Looks shot, but they's thousan's of miles in
her. Lined up side by side. Good Used Cars. Bargains.
Clean, runs good" (<u>Grapes</u> 85).

California, thought by the migrant workers to be
a "Promised Land," really is a "place of new and
cruel tragedy" (Allen 162). Agricultural organization
involved using migratory "fruit tramps," and the
'Okies, in competition with these people, were forced
to live in poverty (Allen 161). Many refugees had to
live in "makeshift Hoovervilles," notes Allen (162).
Steinbeck emphasizes migrant desperation when he
says, "Our people are good people; our people are
kind people. Pray God some day kind people won't all
be poor. Pray God some day a kid can eat" (<u>Grapes</u>
307-08).

Quotations from the novel are examples of primary sources.

In chapter twenty-five of <u>The Grapes of Wrath</u>, Steinbeck describes California's beauty and then moves to the discontent in California: there were a "million people hungry, needing the fruit" because potatoes were dumped in the river, kerosene was put on the oranges, and pigs were made inedible (448). "In the souls of the people the grapes of wrath are filling and growing heavy, growing heavy for the vintage" (<u>Grapes</u> 449).

The time was ripe for new politics to take shape. In <u>The American Political Tradition</u>, Richard Hofstadter states that Roosevelt's New Deal "released the great forces of mass protest. . . [and] established the principle that the entire community through the agency of the federal government has some responsibility for mass welfare. . ." (340).

Theater critic Robert Brustein, reviewing the 1990 Broadway version of <u>The Grapes of Wrath</u>, congratulates Frank Galati and the Steppenwolf company for bringing Steinbeck's message of social reform to a modern audience and feels that the work has value as a fable where "the American family [is] holding together against all odds" (30). Brustein, however, feels that this "mythical evocation" is "of a more innocent age, when our hopes for social reform had not yet foundered on the rocks of violence, greed, and selfishness" (30-31).

Steinbeck won the Nobel Prize for Literature in 1962 for his writing. Steinbeck was well-suited to write this journey of the Okies to California, describing the personal conditions of a fictional family named the Joads. Although Steinbeck has been criticized, one must remember that some of the critics were so concerned with their own vested interests that they could not accept the validity of his work. Steinbeck's work involved his interpretation and presentation of historical events; and, according to social historian Allen, "that struggling army of refugees . . . has been made vivid to hundreds of thousands of readers in Steinbeck's <u>The Grapes of Wrath</u>" (158).

But what is the novel's significance today?

In 1989, oral historian Studs Terkel, who wrote the introduction to the fiftieth-anniversary edition of <u>The Grapes of Wrath</u>, says that there are living parallels today to the Joads of the 1930's in an essay aptly titled "We Still See Their Faces." Terkel calls Steinbeck's book "an anthem in praise of human community" (30). He also notes that it is "the second most banned book in American schools and public libraries" (31) not because of the language but because of its "subversive" nature in standing up for the down-trodden, the migrant, the homeless, the unfortunate--in essence, the unpopular. While the Depression may no longer be with us, some of its worst aspects--oppression and disillusionment--have not disappeared.

Steinbeck's work does indeed reflect the economic and social plight of the Okies during the Great Depression and still is relevant for us today.

Since the author's name is given in the introduction to the quotation, only the page number is needed within the parentheses.

Note

[1]For an account of the "Okies" then and now, consult Gerald Haslam's <u>The Other California: The Great Central Valley in Life and Letters</u>, a collection of nineteen essays by the author. Haslam, a California native and commentator on California culture, points out that "over 350,000 people finally migrated to California from the Okie states" (110). He characterizes the migrants, the "Dust Bowlers," principally from Oklahoma, Texas, Arkansas, and Missouri, but also from many other states, in this way:

> A tough, able people, the Okies have moved a long way from those ditch banks of the 1930s. They are prominent in state and local government, in all professions, and whether they have chosen to join the state's mainstream or remain displaced Southwesterners, they are proud of their survival. The place they settled most densely, the southern end of the Central Valley, has been profoundly altered by their presence. (122)

Student's Name   13

Works Cited

Place work-cited
entries in
alphabetical order
according to the
last name of the
author or, lacking
an author's name,
the first important
word of the title.

Allen, Frederick Lewis. <u>Since Yesterday</u>. New York:

    Bantam, 1961.

Brustein, Robert. "What Makes a Play Live." <u>New

    Republic</u> 7 May 1990: 30-31.

Galbraith, John Kenneth. <u>The Great Crash</u>. 2nd ed.

    Boston: Houghton, 1961.

Haslam, Gerald. <u>The Other California: The Great Cen-

    tral Valley in Life and Letters</u>. Western Litera-

    ture Ser. Reno: U of Nevada P, 1994.

Hochenauer, Kurt. "The Rhetoric of American Protest:

    Thomas Paine and the Education of Tom Joad."

    <u>Midwest Quarterly</u> 35.4 (1994): 392-404.

Hofstadter, Richard. <u>The American Political

    Tradition</u>. New York: Vintage, 1948.

Owens, Louis. The Grapes of Wrath: <u>Trouble in the

    Promised Land</u>. Twayne's Masterwork Studies

    No. 27. Boston: Twayne, 1989.

Steinbeck, Elaine, and Robert Wallsten, eds. <u>Stein-

    beck: A Life in Letters</u>. New York: Viking, 1975.

"Steinbeck." <u>Funk and Wagnalls New Encyclopedia</u>.

    1986 ed.

Student's Name   14

Steinbeck, John. <u>The Grapes of Wrath</u>. 1939. New York:

    Penguin, 1976.

Terkel, Studs. "We Still See Their Faces." <u>New</u>

    <u>Statesman and Society</u> 30 June 1989: 28-31.

Wyatt, David, ed. <u>New Essays on</u> The Grapes of Wrath.

    The American Novel Ser. New York: Cambridge UP,

    1990.

Remove the underline from a title within a title to set if off.

Appendix

Guidelines for the Preparation of Student Papers in APA Style

In its *Publication Manual* (1994), the American Psychological Association makes a distinction between a student paper and a manuscript being submitted to a journal for publication. The requirements for each are slightly different, with the student paper being given more latitude in typography and format. The manuscript prepared for publication must conform to rigid specifications as to spacing, positioning of tables, figures, notes, and so on, since it must go through the intermediate stage of being edited and printed before it reaches the public. Because the student paper is modeled on the paper to be published, it is important, then, first to understand the APA guidelines for the preparation of manuscripts.

The APA divides articles into three types:

1. *Empirical studies:* Papers that explain the researcher's own experiments and observations
2. *Review articles:* Papers that "are critical evaluations of material that has already been published" (p. 5)
3. *Theoretical articles:* Papers that are speculative in nature and present new ideas based on what has gone before

Each of the papers is set up in basically the same form: an *Introduction* (not labeled) consists of an identification of the study, background information, and a purpose statement. Next, the *Method* section (labeled) explains how the research was done, who participated in it, and lists materials used to carry out the study. The *Results* section (labeled) contains the data that support the investigation: statistics, tables, figures. Finally, the *Discussion* section (also labeled) provides the author's conclusions and evaluations.

In a social science-oriented paper, the structure, as described above, allows readers to comprehend the material more efficiently than if a standard format were not used, and readers accustomed to this uniformity of design are able to follow along expectantly as a problem is presented and a solution given. It should be kept in mind, though, that the APA form is best suited for papers that are more data-intensive than, say, an MLA paper that is more explicative and where numerical data play little part in the analysis of the topic. Thus, APA style is more suited to topics like number 2 in Chapter 2 (chart the laugh opportunities on a program like *Seinfeld*) where you can set up the paper into the Method, Results, and Discussion sections and provide your findings in a readily accessible format. The APA format would also work well with topic 4 (what makes a fad catch on?); topic 5 (explore the types and themes of children's books); topic 20 (account for the decline of Western movies); topic 21 (explain the mathematical frequency of coincidence); topic 27 (analyze the advertising in various media); topic 28 (study the population of a locale); topic 29 (analyze the popularity of names); topic 31 (what does it mean to be middle class?); topic 35 (evaluate the movie rating system); topic 36 (how well is a law observed?); topic 37 (map the frequency, intensity, and duration of aggression on a TV program); topic 39 (how does television affect behavior?); topic 45 (explain the principles of Total Quality Management); topic 47 (account for the fast-food phenomenon) and others.

As we shall see, the APA citation and reference system differs from the MLA system in some basic ways. One way is in the APA's use of headings to divide up the material of the paper. (The MLA uses no headings.) The basic division of Method, Results and Discussion can be further divided depending on the length and complexity of the subject. The APA has a system of five levels of headings for the most complex material:

1. centered upper case and lower case letters
2. centered and underlined upper case and lower case letters
3. flush left and underlined upper case and lower case letters
4. indented and underlined lower case letters ending with a period
5. centered capitals

For short papers, only one level is used: centered upper case and lower case letters. Headings are, of course, dividers and correspond to the lettered and numbered divisions of outlines.

Although both systems provide essentially the same information for the researcher, they do it in different ways. As you look at the same entry in both systems, you will notice that the APA system places the year in a prominent position since the recency of the research is always important in empirical studies, whereas the meaning of a short story will not change over the years even though the interpretations may.

The APA book and periodical references that follow can be compared to their MLA counterparts in Chapter Six.

Book with Single Author

APA Reference List Entry

```
Petroski, H. (1992). The evolution of useful things. New
    York: Knopf.
```

In the above APA Reference list entry, the surname comes first, followed by the author's initials; the date of publication is given in parentheses; the title, underlined, follows with only the first word and proper nouns and adjectives capitalized; the city of publication comes next followed by the two-letter postal designation for the state (except that Boston, New York, Philadelphia, Baltimore, Chicago, Los Angeles, and San Francisco do not require a state designation after them because they are well-known publishing centers); the publisher's name follows in simplified form.

The first line of the entry above would be indented five to seven spaces as in a paragraph (in a student paper, however, the entry could also be set as a hanging indent, as in the MLA format).

Here are two examples of how the Petroski source might be used in the text of a paper:

APA In-text Citation

- We often take common objects for granted and are surprised to find out that, for example, "not until the seventeenth century did the fork appear in England" (Petroski, 1992, p.8).

- Henry Petroski (1992) points out that "not until the seventeenth century did the fork appear in England" (p.8).

Here is the Petroski source presented in MLA format:

MLA Works-Cited Entry

```
Petroski, Henry. The Evolution of Useful Things. New York:
     Knopf, 1992.
```

MLA In-text Citation

- We often take common objects for granted and are surprised to find out that, for example, "not until the seventeenth century did the fork appear in England" (Petroski 8).

- Henry Petroski points out that "not until the seventeenth century did the fork appear in England" (8).

Book with Multiple Authors

APA Reference List Entry

```
Strunk, W., Jr. & White, E.B. (1979). The elements of style
     (3rd ed.) New York: Macmillan.
```

APA In-text Citation

- Strunk and White stress the importance of creating word pictures: "If those who have studied the art of writing are in accord on any one point, it is on this: the surest way to arouse and hold the attention of the reader is by being specific, definite, and concrete" (p. 21).

Or, as in the above citation for one author, the reference can come after the quotation:

- Creating word pictures is an important part of effective writing: "If those who have studied the art of writing are in accord on any one point, it is on this: the surest way to arouse and hold the attention of the reader is by being specific, definite, and concrete" (Strunk & White, 1979, p. 21).

Three to Five Authors

- The world bird population has been estimated at 100 billion by Robbins, Bruun, and Zim (1966).

In the in-text citation, all authors are listed up to six; with six or more use the first author's surname and et al.: (Smythe, et al., 1994).

Book with Group Author

```
Cleveland State University. (1992). Annual report of philan-
     thropy. Cleveland, OH: Author.
```

[In the APA format, when the publisher is the same entity as the author, then the word *Author* is used to replace the duplication of the publisher's name.]

Edited Book

Beck, H. P. (1968). Where the workers of the world unite. In T. P. Coffin (Ed.), <u>Our living traditions: An introduction to folklore</u> (pp. 58-69). New York: Basic Books.

Reference Book

<u>American Heritage Dictionary</u> (2nd college ed.)(1983). Boston: Houghton Mifflin.

Onions, C.T. (Ed.).(1966). <u>The Oxford Dictionary of English Etymology</u>. New York: Oxford University Press.

<u>Chicago Manual of Style</u> (1982). (13th ed.) Chicago: University of Chicago Press.

Landis, F. (1986). Vapor. In <u>Funk and Wagnalls new encyclopedia</u>. (Vol. 26, pp. 408-409). New York: Funk and Wagnalls.

Brochure or Pamphlet

International Visitors Committee. (1990). <u>Tips for receiving international business and professional visitors: A brief guide to customs and expectations of travelers from abroad</u>. Cleveland, OH: Cleveland Council on World Affairs.

Periodical

Anderson, K. (1994, July 3). Archives combed for Cherokee ties. <u>Dallas Morning News</u>, pp. 49A, 52A.

Schlack, L. B. (1992, November) School days [Letter to the Editor]. <u>World Monitor</u>, p. 5.

Rybczynski, W. (1993, May). The new downtowns. <u>The Atlantic Monthly</u>, 271.5, 98-106.

Angell, R. (1993, May 3). Put me in, Coach. <u>The New Yorker</u>, 47-56, 61-62.

Jenkyns, R. (1993, May 10). Hat trick. [Review of the book *The man in the bowler hat*]. <u>The New Yorker</u>, 109-112.

Tobin, G. A. (1968). The bicycle boom of the 1890's: The development of private transportation and the birth of the modern tourist. <u>Journal of popular culture</u>, 7.4, 838-849.

Sample Paper APA Style

APA Style: Begin a page with a title or chapter heading at least an inch and a half from the top. Left margins are one and a half inches; bottom, top, and right at least an inch.

Understanding Spatial Relationships

Between Peoples of Different Cultures

Because commerce is becoming more international (as demonstrated by the linguistic shorthand of the times: NAFTA, GATT, G-7) those engaged in the manufacture and sale of products need to understand not only foreign languages but also other countries' customs and behaviors. Indeed, anyone open to the complexities of modern information sharing will benefit from a closer look at how our social behavior communicates messages in ways different from speech but in ways no less important.

Distances that separate conversing individuals vary from culture to culture. Desmond Morris (1977) points out that "we all carry with us, everywhere we go, a portable territory called a Personal Space. If people move inside the space, we feel threatened. If they keep too far outside it, we feel rejected" (p. 99). Western Europeans converse at "fingertip distance," Eastern Europeans at "wrist distance," and Mediterraneans at "elbow distance" (Morris, p. 100).

Edward T. Hall and Mildred Reed Hall (1987) explain the concept of spatial distancing with a bubble metaphor:

> In northern Europe, the bubbles [personal spaces] are quite large; moving south to France, Italy, Greece, and Spain, the bubbles get smaller and smaller so that the distance that is perceived as intimate in the north overlaps personal distances in the south, which means that Mediterranean Europeans "get too close" to the Germans, the English, and Americans of northern European ancestry. (p. 13)

However, in Latin America the distances are even closer: "A Venezuelan may stand as close as four to eight inches away" (International Visitors Committee, 1990, p. 19). According to Hall (1959), because the conversational spatial ranges for Latin Americans are so different, Latin Americans may think that North Americans are "distant or cold, withdrawn and unfriendly" (p. 185). North Americans, in contrast, may feel that Latin Americans are encroaching on their territory, and the North Americans, without realizing it, may start edging backward (Hall, 1959).

APA Style: Page header consists of two or three words of the title, five spaces, and then the page number. Position these about one-half inch from the top.

Not only do distances differ among peoples, but language behaviors themselves vary from place to place, and what we ourselves perceive as alien and even uncomfortable may be the normal mode of behavior for others. In Finland, for example, eye contact is an important aspect of communications; in Zimbabwe, it is considered rude (International Visitors Committee, 1990, pp. 24, 42). In Albania and Bulgaria, according to the same source, communicating with traditional head signals may cause a visitor confusion since in those countries "head motions bear extra notice: a nod up and down means 'no,' while a sideward shake means 'yes'" (p. 33).

Now, as we enter the twenty-first century, electronic communication protocols are changing the way we interact with each other even more. Douglas A. Brent (1994), for example, argues that the new information revolution, including emerging technologies of electronic mail, hypertext, interactive video, and networking, will break down barriers between academic disciplines just as television broke down barriers between an elite culture and an informal culture by creating a homogenous middle ground available to both. He points out that unlike traditional information exchanges that have heretofore maintained their separateness in the academic world (informal discussions vs. formal conferences vs. refereed journals, for instance), the new electronic information exchanges are less formal, less compartmentalized, less rigid, and less bounded by traditional communications conventions such as space and time.

Thus, distances--whether face to face or in cyberspace--have their own sets of rules that can change depending on the physical location of the medium of communication used. Our awareness of these distancing mechanisms can help us to optimize the communication process itself or to minimize the impact of those things that separate us as individuals in the modern world. We must, then, acculturate ourselves to the ways of others in order to communicate effectively and to get along peaceably.

Understanding Spatial Relationships   4

References

Brent, D.A. (1994, December). Information technology

and the breakdown of "places" of knowledge. [31

paragraphs] <u>EJournal</u> [On-line serial], <u>4</u>

(4). Available: LISTSERVE@ALBANY.edu

Hall, E. T. (1959/1973). <u>The silent language</u>. New

York: Doubleday/Anchor Books.

Hall, E. T. & Hall, M. R. (1987). <u>Hidden differences:</u>

<u>Doing business with the Japanese</u>. New York:

Doubleday/Anchor Books.

International Visitors Committee.(1990). <u>Tips for</u>

<u>receiving international business and profes-</u>

<u>sional visitors: A brief guide to customs and</u>

<u>expectations of travelers from abroad</u>. Cleve-

land, OH: Cleveland Council on World Affairs.

Morris, D. (1977). <u>Manwatching: A field guide to</u>

<u>human behavior</u>. New York: Abrams.